Viewer Beware!

The *Goosebumps* TV Companion

by

Jose Prendes

BearManor Media

Orlando, Florida

Viewer Beware! The Goosebumps TV Companion
© 2020 Jose Prendes. All Rights Reserved.

No portion of this publication may be reproduced, stored, and/or copied electronically (except for academic use as a source), nor transmitted in any form or by any means without the prior written permission of the publisher and/or author.

Published in the USA by
BearManor Media
1317 Edgewater Dr. #110
Orlando, FL 32804
www.BearManorMedia.com

Softcover Edition
ISBN: 978-1-62933-612-1

Printed in the United States of America

Table of Contents

-Season One (Episodes 1-19)   1
-Season Two (Episodes 20-44)   55
-Season Three (Episodes 45-66)   111
-Season Four (Episodes 67-74)   163
-Talking 'Bumps: Interview with the cast & Crew   185
-Appendix 1: Interview with superfan ZakBabyTV   209
-Special Thanks   215

For

Rembo,

No longer scared of needles.

&

Crabby,

No longer scared of anything.

"Viewers beware, you're in for a scare."

-R.L. Stine, opening of series

SEASON ONE

<u>Original Airdate:</u>

October 27, 1995 - May 17, 1996

EP.1:
"The Haunted Mask Pt. 1"
<u>Airdate</u>: October 27, 1995
<u>Written by</u>: Jose Rivera
<u>Directed by</u>: Timothy Bond
<u>Based on the Goosebumps book</u>: The Haunted Mask (#11)

Guest Cast

Kathryn Long	Colin Fox
Kathryn Short	Brenda Bazinet

Favorite Line:
"Last summer they put that dead octopus on me."
-Carly Beth

Synopsis
Carly Beth, beleaguered scaredy cat, decides to pay a couple of bullies back and finds a really scary mask to wear for Halloween to give them a taste of their own medicine, but discovers the mask is more than she bargained for.

Review
Adapting the eleventh Goosebumps novel, the series kicks off with a bang here. This episode really sets the template and tone for how the series will proceed and how the novels will eventually be retrofitted for TV purposes. Not a lot of time is wasted getting to the good stuff, even with a 2-part runtime, and we are given enough save-the-cat moments with Carly Beth (Kathryn Long) where we really find ourselves on her side.

Early on, we meet the bullies Chuck and Steve, who jump out of a pumpkin patch in the middle of the night to scare Carly Beth and her pal Sabrina (Kathryn Short), but I wonder how long those goofballs were waiting for under all those leaves with pumpkins on their heads? We later meet her annoying brother Noah, and her mom who has for some reason made a plaster of Paris model of Carly Beth's face. That mask smiles to Carly

Beth, and later to the camera (basically us), but that doesn't make any sense within the logic of this particular episode, because the mask of Carly Beth isn't haunted, so what the hell is going on there? We will never know.

And the haunted mask itself, you ask? Well, she finds it in the boringly-titled Novelty Store, run by an unnamed fellow that is credited as Tall Thin Man (Colin Fox). Having found nothing truly terrifying on the store shelves, she sneaks into the back while he's yelling into his phone that he doesn't care about the customers. She finds a row of freaky masks, each grotesque in its own ways, and is smitten, for lack of a better word, with the demonic-looking one. The Tall Thin Man refuses to sell it, so she does what any kid would do: she throws up a random amount of money and runs out of the store with it. The mask has already begun to corrupt her!

This episode works really well because Kathryn Long does a great job of portraying Carly Beth as a relatable and sympathetic girl. I wish more had been done with the mysterious shop owner, similar to Sardo in *Are You Afraid of the Dark?*, but the writers had to stay within the confines of Mister Stine's book, so I understand. The episode comes to a crashing halt as Sabrina, dressed as some kind of rodent, confronts Carly Beth about the fearsomeness of the mask and Carly Beth freaks out on her as it fades to black. I realize this was considered a one-hour episode, but I would have liked a more definitive cliffhanger, because this is just too vague of an ending, especially if someone were to watch it out of order on TV sometime.

Series Mythology

-The pilot, suitably debuting the series during Halloween, is the first of sixteen one-hour (two-part) episodes.

-This episode breaks some kind of cosmic rule, because the two female leads are BOTH named Kathryn, and that's not all! Kathryn LONG plays Carly Beth and Kathryn SHORT plays Sabrina. Holy moly! Mind blown, right?

-"The Haunted Mask" is writer Jose Rivera's only brush with the show.

He is best remembered as co-creator and writer for the spiritually similar kids' series *Eerie, Indiana* in 1991.

-This is the first of six episodes that director Timothy Bond will helm. Technically it's 3 episodes, because they were all two-parters.

-This episode is introduced Rod Serling style by R.L. Stine himself.

-Kathryn Long insisted on using a real worm for reality-sake during the worm-in-the-tune-sandwich scene. That's some serious commitment.

-Apparently Mr. Stine cameos among the trick or treaters, and my daughter swears she saw his mask among the masks in the Novelty Shop, but I combed through this episode and couldn't find it, so there is a hidden Easter Egg in this one!

EP.2:
"The Haunted Mask Pt. 2"

<u>Airdate:</u> October 27, 1995
<u>Written by:</u> Jose Rivera
<u>Directed by:</u> Timothy Bond
<u>Based on the Goosebumps book:</u> The Haunted Mask (#11)

Guest Cast

Kathryn Long	Colin Fox
Kathryn Short	Brenda Bazinet

Favorite Line:
"What are you supposed to be, a giant hamster?"
-Some Random Kid

Synopsis

The plight of Carly Beth and her haunted mask continues as she accomplishes her mission and terrorizes the bullies that have been bothering her for years, only to find out that the mask won't come off afterwards and she may have to grow accustomed to a new, hideous face.

Review

We meet up with moron duo Chuck and Steve, dressed as pirates of course. They're singing sea shanties in a cemetery, because that's what cool kids do apparently. Carly Beth, now a full demon, or whatever she is supposed to be, tracks them down and manages to scare them as planned. However, they know it's her immediately, which really doesn't make much sense, and kind of makes the mask pointless if they know it's her already. She still wields a power over them and forces them to their knees where she makes them beg forgiveness for all their trespasses against her. At this point the plaster head starts asking for help, they freak, and run off. The demon Carly Beth then proceeds to bury her plaster head in the grave soil, putting to rest the old CB for good.

Here is where the episode, and by association this two-parter, takes a really disappointing turn, because when she runs into Sabrina again, Carly snaps out of her haunted trance or what-have-you and returns to Sabrina's house to eat candy. What the heck? Wasn't the mask in full control already? How is she able to just snap out of it? Anyway, she tries to take it off and finds that the mask has fused with her skin, and it sends her running back to the Novelty Shop for help.

The Tall Thin Man can't help her, but the episode rights itself when he reveals that he can't take off the mask, because it isn't a mask, it's a real face! Say what? Then he reveals that they were all HIS face at one point or another and he's wearing one right now that is slowly decaying as well. I wonder what he looks like without the mask, because sadly we never find out, and in a way I like that bit of mystery. The guy tells her that a token of love might be able to break the spell, but before we get more details on how the masks were created and how this magic skin works, the remaining skin masks start floating in the air with some really dodgy special effects and they chase Carly Beth out into the night.

She gets the bright idea to run into the cemetery and finds herself at the spot where she buried the plaster of Paris head her mom lovingly sculpted for her. Isn't that a coincidence, folks? She digs it up as the floating masks dance around her in the dark and she shows them the Carly Beth head, which somehow scares the living heck out of the masks and they fly away goofily. Carly tries to remove the mask once again and it works, she's free! She returns home to give her mom a big hug and thank her for the life-saving face sculpt she made, only to turn around and find that her jerky brother has slipped the haunted mask on, continuing the curse.

The episode ends here, and it is a righteous finale, because it's a solid down-beat ending and in a way her jerky brother is getting repaid for his behavior by being cursed as well. Again Kathryn Long does a wonderful job of playing up Carly Beth's desperation, despite the fact that she is in a mask for almost the entire episode. The wicked reveal about the mask's origins was incredibly bizarre and creepy, and I wish it had been expounded upon in later iterations of Goosebumps. This second half also felt longer and denser than the first half, but all in all, this was a solid one-hour episode, however the parts by themselves don't hold up on their own.

<u>Series Mythology</u>

-Kathryn Long and Colin Fox return as Carly Beth and the Shopkeeper, respectively, in season two's "The Haunted Mask 2".

-Kathryn Short's Sabrina will also return for the sequel, but we will see her again before that at the end of season one in another two-parter, "A Night in Terror Tower".

-Brenda Bazinet, Carly Beth's Mom, Cody Jones, Carly Beth's brother Noah, and Amos Crawley, who played Chuck, will also return in the sequel a year later.

-George Kinamis, who played Steve Boswell, will not return to reprise his character in the sequel, where actor John White plays Steve, but we will meet this actor first in the next episode, where he battles against a tricky Cuckoo clock!

EP.3:
"The Cuckoo Clock of Doom"

<u>Airdate</u>: November 3, 1995

<u>Written by</u>: Billy Brown & Dan Angel

<u>Directed by</u>: John Bell

<u>Based on the Goosebumps book</u>: The Cuckoo Clock of Doom (#28)

Guest Cast

John White	Kristen Bone
Cynthia Belliveau	Larry Mannell

Favorite Line:

"What a Kerj. I told you he was a Krej. That's jerk spelled backwards, you Krej!"

-Tara Webster, Mean Little Sister

Synopsis

When Michael Webster messes with his family's mysterious, new cuckoo clock, time itself being to mess with him.

Review

Poor Michael. Talk about beleaguered underdogs. Forget Rocky, or Kevin McCallister, Michael is the true downtrodden, sad sack hero we've all been looking for. His horrible, sociopathic sister Tara torments and embarrasses him on a daily basis, and their wimpy mom is too blind to see any of it, despite her massive glasses. Tara squirts fake blood all over him and blames Michael for it. She trips him at his birthday party and he falls face first into his cake in front of the girl he's crushing on. Also, she calls him a Krej! Again, I reiterate, poor Michael. He needs some magic Goosebumps craziness to deliver him from this torturous hell, and into a kinder hell.

That magic comes in the form of a Cuckoo Clock. How? Why? I'll let Michael's dad explain: "Well, the legend is that a strange, old man built the clock over a hundred years ago and he put a magical spell on it. But they say whoever discovers the magic must beware." Admittedly, not much to go on, but obviously no one believes it anyway. Michael sees the clock as a way to get his bratty sister in trouble, and later that night he sneaks downstairs and twists the neck on the creepy little cuckoo bird that pops out. This, of course, is how the magic is discovered, and Michael is now in temporal hot water, because time is looking for revenge.

Not only does he relive his traumatic twelfth birthday party, but he has a rather goofy nightmare of running down a green screen hallway, being chased by the giant cuckoo clock, only to have Tara's laughing head explode out from where the cuckoo bird would exit! The next day isn't any better, because he wakes up as a six-year-old, and here the producers manage to throw in a fun nod to *Home Alone*. He quickly makes the obvious conclusion that time is going backwards, and since he twisted the cuckoo bird's head around backwards, it all starts to make sense… in a Goosebumps way. Once he realizes how to solve his predicament, it's already too late, because at this point in his timeline the clock is back in the antique store, and no matter how proactive he tries to be, time is not on his side.

Facing extinction at the hands of time, he awakens on the third day as a baby! The worst things about this iteration of his personal hell are the wigs the actors who play his parents have to wear to look younger. Somehow he gets them to take him to the antique store, where his parents proceed to abandon their year-old baby in a stroller and do some antiquing! Of course, this gives our hero a chance to reach for the cuckoo bird in the clock and set forward the hands of time. Like a scene from the improbable *Baby's Day Out*, baby Michael climbs up a tower of furniture to get to the clock and I should mention that the clock has numbers from one to hundred along the sides and he knocks off the eighty-eight by accident during said climb, remember that. Anyway, he manages to turn the cuckoo bird's head back around to normal, which doesn't make sense because it wasn't backwards in the past, but I'll let it slide because we're playing with Goosebumps rules.

The spell is broken and time is restored. He returns to his young-grunge twelve-year-old self, but there is one major difference with this new timeline. The eighty-eight he knocked off was the year Tara would have been born, and since it no longer exists on the clock, Tara no longer exists; only he remembers her. He assumes there is some way to go back and fix it, restore her into existence, but he's in no hurry and the episode fades out on his creepy, joyful smile. Now THAT is how you end an episode!

This is a pretty solid, fast-paced episode. No time is wasted and every second is packed with either plot or character development. Writers Brown and Angel do a bang up job condensing the book and delivering a high-stakes episode with a very likable hero, and Tara is certainly evil enough to not only make the setup work well, but allow the ending to be extra sweet, despite it's darker implications. This is one of my all-time favorites for sure.

<u>Series Mythology</u>

-As stated in the last episode, John White (Michael), will return in season two's "The Haunted Mask 2".

-This is the first episode written by Executive Story Editors Billy Brown and Dan Angel, who would become the most prolific writers on the series with a total of thirty-six episodes.

-This is director John Bell's first of seven episodes that he will be directing for the series. In fact, he'll be directing the next episode as well, "The Girl Who Cried Monster".

-In this episode Michael and his dad are pouring over a ton of Clifford, The Big Red Doc books, but why would they feature another book franchise in a Goosebumps TV series? Simple, both are owned by the Scholastic Corporation and equally beloved by their respective fans.

EP.4:
"The Girl Who Cried Monster"
Airdate: November 10, 1995
Written by: Charles Lazer
Directed by: John Bell
Based on the Goosebumps book: The Girl Who Cried Monster (#8)

Guest Cast

Eugene Lipinski	Deborah Scorsone
Christopher Tuah	Lynne Cormack

Favorite Line:
"No! My parents aren't home right now. I mean, they'll be home any minute. I mean, they're in the bathroom. Mom, is dad still cleaning his rifle?"
-Lucy Dark

Synopsis
Lucy Dark is a young R.L. Stine in training, but when she discovers that her favorite librarian is a bug-eyed, insect-eating alien creature, the horror becomes too real; in fact, it becomes a threat to her and her family's very existence.

Review
Lucy is my kind of girl. Who doesn't love to scare people? It's a riot! She's also a bookworm, and good for her she chooses yummy reads like *Frankenstein*. Her librarian is a suitably creepy dude, too. Mr. Morton's library is an imposing, gothic castle, complete with random cat jump scares! It's revealed early on in this ridiculously fast paced episode that not only is he creepy, but he's a monster! I'm pretty sure actor Eugene Lipinski, Mr. Mortman himself, actually did eat a mouthful of crickets, continuing with the actor commitment we saw from Kathryn Long and the live worm in the pilot episode.

I mentioned the fast pace, and what I mean by that is that once Mortman's true identity is discovered by Lucy, not much interplay time is spent on the cat and mouse scenarios that would have accompanied say a feature length version. I'm reminded of that amazing 80s classic *Fright Night* here, except in super-truncated form. Of course, it does have to fit into a twenty-two-minute runtime for television (got to pack in those commercials, kids!), but I felt the episode "Cuckoo Clock of Doom" used its small timeframe effectively. Here, things spin out of control fast and come to dead man's curve (pun intended) rather quickly. Before, we know it, the trouble has been solved, and a new reality is presented to the audience for it to digest.

Goosebumps is known for it's twist endings and last-minute reversals of fortune, but this early episode in the life of the series is really the best of the best when it comes to those mechanics. When Lucy's disbelieving folks reveal themselves as snake monsters and begin to devour Mr. Mortman, we realize all along we've been conned, but in an oh-so-satisfying way. There is nothing better than having a TV show or a movie be smarter than you. Watching this episode again is a worthy endeavor, because every interchange between Lucy and her family takes on another, richer meaning, and Lynn Cormack & Dan Lett, who play her mom and dad respectively, really shine as they tow the line between seeming like the disinterested parents indulging in a kid's imagination, and monsters in disguise making sure their territory stays clear of competition.

This one is a joy to watch because not only does it go at a break-neck speed, but it's very satisfying. Not much is known about Mr. Mortman's origins, much less the origins of Lucy's snake family, but in a way that's a better, creepier direction to take this than filling it with wordy exposition. The mysterious always works best when it stays mysterious. I say, leave the shadows alone.

<u>Series Mythology</u>

-This is writer Charles Lazer's first of nine episodes that he will write for the series.

-Actor Eugene Lipinski, who played Mr. Mortman, will return to the series in voice only in season two's "Night of The Living Dummy 3" as Slappy's puppet sidekick, Rocky.

-Despite having unique surnames, actor Brandon Bone, who played Randy in this episode, and actor Kristen Bone, who played Tara last episode, are NOT related. Keeping with that, Eugene Lipinski is also NOT related to *Are You Afraid of the Dark?* star and future figure skater, Tara Lipinski.

-Contrary to popular belief, the "Razor-Toothed Toe-Biter" is not real. I know, I know, I'm bummed, too.

EP.5:
"Welcome to Camp Nightmare Pt.1"

<u>Airdate</u>: November 17, 1995
<u>Written by</u>: Jeffrey "Jeff" Cohen
<u>Directed by</u>: Ron Oliver
<u>Based on the Goosebumps book</u>: <u>Welcome to Camp Nightmare</u> (#9)

Guest Cast

Kaj-Erik Eriksen	Chris Benson
Jeffrey Akomah	Benjamin Plener

Favorite Line:

"Nightmoon, oh, Nightmoon, our hearts are full of pride.
Nightmoon, oh, Nightmoon, Uncle Al will be our guide.
Coddlers and whiners, they are not welcome here.
Nightmoon's for big guys, there is no place for fear!"
-Camp Nightmoon Anthem

Synopsis

Welcome to Camp Nightmoon, an idyllic, secluded summer camp where you can play some baseball, roast marshmallows, go on hikes, and also get stalked by a hungry werewolf named Sabre.

Review

    This episode has everything! Explosions! Monsters! Campers! Guys named Al! However, at the same time, this episode has nothing. It's almost all first-act material with time and suspense being wasted on trying to build up the subpar camp counselor Larry as the villain. We see the damn monster in the opening sequence, we know it's real, or I should say "real", so Larry is a total red herring and it just sucks the tension out of the first-half for me, with the focus moving toward him and his annoying antics.

    Uncle Al, and just to clarify he's not related to anyone, draws attention to something called the "forbidden bunk", which naturally becomes the obsession of everyone at camp, but muddles the proceedings. Balancing the mysterious bunk and the Sabre monster really becomes difficult, as they don't necessarily seem to be related. In fact, the first camper to disappear mysteriously is bitten by a snake, a legitimate threat, and that is basically all of the dramatic thrust for this episode, which connects to neither of our perceived evils.

Our hero Billy, self-appointed mama bear to his bunkmates, mentions that his folks are scientists and go on trips a lot, which hints at the last-minute twist reveal coming in the second-half of this two-parter. It's a subtle nod, but I like it because it adds a bit of depth when viewed a second time around. Beyond that, this first-half is a bit of a snooze, because we are given so much to worry about, but at the same time too little to care for. Needless to say, it doesn't stand on its own, and obviously it wasn't meant to, I just wish they had done something more with the lore here instead of wasting it on tedious filler moments like the baseball game. However, I will revisit this episode when we discuss the next episode and view it as a whole.

Series Mythology

-This is director Ron Oliver's first of sixteen episodes for *Goosebumps*, coming close to matching the seventeen episodes he directed for *Are You Afraid of the Dark?* However, he only wrote two episodes of *Dark*, but beat that record on this series by writing seven episodes of *Goosebumps*.

-Writer Jeff Cohen's first of two (technically three) scripts. He will return to write season two's "Ghost Beach".

-It's also worth noting that this is ONLY time in the series when the *Goosebumps* books were adapted in order, with last episode's "The Girl Who Cried Monster" being book #8 and this one being book #9.

EP.6:
"Welcome to Camp Nightmare Pt.2"

<u>Airdate</u>: November 24, 1995

<u>Written by</u>: Jeffrey "Jeff" Cohen

<u>Directed by</u>: Ron Oliver

<u>Based on the Goosebumps book</u>: Welcome to Camp Nightmare (#9)

Guest Cast

Ken Mundy	Paul Brogren
David Roemmele	Sarah Mitchell

Favorite Line:

"Research tells us the aliens there are pretty dangerous and, uh, unpredictable."

-Billy's Dad

Synopsis

Billy continues to face off against the nightmares of Camp Nightmoon, testing his fortitude and bravery as he searches for an answer to all the strangeness.

Review

    The second half of this episode is in some regards more interesting, but still not enough. The muddled mess adds fuel to the fire when two of Billy's pals drown in the lake and since it can't be chalked up to either the forbidden bunk or Sabre, it becomes evident that the whole camp is just a series of pitfalls and blind alleys of bad luck. In a sense, this cements the threat as not just being a monster or a haunted cabin or whatever, but an overall threat. Some clever editing makes Billy's transition from confused and hopeless to brave and fearless fun and adds some life to the proceedings, however that doesn't really help this episode rise to a stirring conclusion.

    For some unknown reason, Billy decides to take matters into his own hands and enter the forbidden bunk, which up to now has been fairly innocuous, and there he meets Dawn, one of the kids from the girl's camp. She's on the run and hiding out there, because the same things are happening in her camp. One moment in the forbidden bunk stands out as particularly bizarre: a strange noise draws Billy and Dawn's attention to a sack of letters, and while rifling through the unsent letters from the campers, Dawn comments that some of these are from years ago. First of all, how do letters make a noise, and second of all, Dawn cannot possibly know how old the letters are. They don't look aged and no one puts the year on the envelope. I know it's nitpicky, but stuff like this adds up when nothing else is there to cover it over it.

As soon as Billy finally takes charge and starts to uncover the secrets, the episode comes to a sharp finale as it's revealed that the camp is actually a top-secret government lab, and Billy was being tested. Oh, boy. Everyone, including the kids who disappeared or where "killed", were actors; they were testing Billy to see how he would handle himself in a crazy situation like the one he was presented. Given that info, I forgive some of the muddled moments, but I still think the pacing was off on this one. Incidentally, Sabre was just an animatronic werewolf head; a pretty sweet one, actually. It looked like they spend a ton of money on it, so I'm surprised they didn't use it more because even in broad daylight it looked really great.

And why was Billy being tested? Simple. He's an alien. They ALL are. parents are being sent on a dangerous exploration mission to Earth and they wanted to make sure he could handle himself there. You know, because on Earth we have werewolves and jerky camp counselors running rampant. This twist, despite the odd logic flaw here and there, is the two-parter's only saving grace, because without it there would be nothing to write home about (see what I did there?).

Series Mythology

-Actors Kaj-Erik Eriksen (Billy), Benjamin Plener (Roger), and Kerry Duff (Dori) also appeared in episodes of *Are You Afraid of the Dark?* Plener double-dipped in both shows with two episodes in *Dark* and appearing in *Goosebumps* again in season three's "The Haunted House Game". Duff only got a second helping of *Bumps* by appearing later this season in the classic "Night of the Living Dummy 2".

-Actors David Roemmele (Mike) and Paul Brogren (Larry) will return to the series. We will see Roemmele again in season three's "Perfect School", and Brogan in this season's "Say Cheese and Die".

EP.7:
"Phantom of the Auditorium"

Airdate: December 1, 1995
Written by: Bruce Edwards
Directed by: John Bell
Based on the Goosebumps book: Phantom of the Auditorium (#24)

Guest Cast

Jessica Moyes	Shawn Potter
Kathryn Greenwood	Stuart Stone

Favorite Line:
"Break a leg, Brooke, as they say."
-Tina

Synopsis
A school's production of *The Phantom of the Opera* is threatened when a masked man similar to the play's Phantom starts to stalk Brooke, the star of the show.

Review
There is A LOT to unpack in this episode, which delivers not one, but two red herrings, and a last minute reveal that just confuses the whole thing. In a way it's similar to "Welcome to Camp Nightmare", where there is so much going on that none of it actually congeals into a straight out plot, but a series of bluffs.

Okay, we have a central plot line, the production of the school play, but we have three villains, for lack of a better word, and they are the jealous understudy Tina, who wants the lead role, the hobo dressing as the phantom and living under the stage, and Brian Colson, the new kid who is actually the ghost of the boy who was supposed to play the phantom 72 years ago and is now back to reclaim his place among the footlights. None of them are connected, but interestingly enough at one point they all seem to be working together. This may get complicated, believe it or not, so let's break down a key sequence to see if we can't dissect it all.

During a rehearsal, Tina tells Brooke, our heroine, that she should "break a leg", and of course this means luck, but the way Tina means it is anything but. On stage, while Brooke and her scene partner are in dramatic ecstasy, the lights go out and the phantom appears on the catwalk. He swings down like Tarzan and warns Brooke to go away, and then disappears through the trapdoor on stage. Suddenly, a prop door falls from the rafters and nearly flattens our lead actress, but Brooke rolls out of the way. On that door is another warning, written in red paint, instructing Esmeralda, in this case Brooke, to stay away. Zeke, who is playing the Phantom in the play, arrives then. He gets blamed by his teacher, but states that it wasn't him because he was at a dentist appointment, which is untrue, because we just saw him at his locker a few scenes ago, and if time isn't being monkeyed with here then Brooke talking to Zeke at his locker was on the same day as all this rigmarole. Then Tina arrives, adding confusion to the fire, and states that the red paint leaves a trail and we should follow it to see who might have been responsible. Tina is suspicious as hell here, but they follow the paint and it leads right to Zeke's locker, which means someone is framing him, and that someone can be none other than Brian, the actual phantom.

So what just happened? Here is where all the plotlines converge in a soup of perfect coincidences, inadvertently putting all of Brooke's enemies in on the same plan. Here's what I think happened: The hobo guy turned the lights off, dressed as the phantom, and swung down to scare Brooke. Tina, who we last saw suspiciously heading up into the rafters after wishing Brooke the ominous "break a leg" comment, lets loose the prop door and tried to take out Brooke so she could be the star of the show. Brian, who had been painting sets and had access to all that gear, wrote the blood red message on the door. It was in his best interests to get Zeke in trouble so he could step into the role of the phantom. Why is this breakdown important? Well, it's either brilliant plotting or an example of confused blind alleys plot-wise. Since, the confluence of events wasn't explored for their coincidental manner,

I am going to lean toward blind alleys, which makes this a frustrating episode. Quickly after this, the hobo is discovered under the stage and run off by the police, Tina's jealousy is diffused and forgotten, and Brian knocks Zeke out and takes his place on stage as the phantom, where he explains how he died on his opening night long ago: "…one hour before the curtain was to rise, I fell into the abyss, where I became a real phantom." He is easily defeated by Brooke when she removes his mask to reveal Brian's normal, unscarred face, and he falls backwards into the trapdoor which has somehow opened up again after just rising up to deposit him on stage.

That's it. End of episode, folks. I know *Goosebumps* is known for its twist endings, but I think all those twists and bluffs really adversely affect the plot, delivering sometimes, not always, but sometimes, a really confused and unsatisfying narrative because we are given nothing to hang our hat on and feel more like pinballs than avid spectators. We didn't need the hobo under the stage subplot, and we also could have used more of Tina's jealousy, but alas all we get is mishmash.

I'm also not sure why they changed *The Phantom of the Opera's* lead character's name from Christine in the original book to Esmeralda, who was Quasimodo's love interest in *The Hunchback of Notre Dame*. At one moment in the aftermath of the scene described in detail above, the drama teacher throws up her hands and says "what a mess", and I have to agree.

Series Mythology

-Writer Bruce Edwards' first of two episodes for the series. He will go on to write this season's "Say Cheese and Die".

-Actor Shawn Potter (Zeke), Stuart Stone (Brian), and Erik Fink (Emile) will not be seen in this series again, but all will appear in *Are You Afraid of the Dark?* Mr. Potter alone appears a whopping three times.

-Actor Julia (aka Julie Annis) Chantrey (Tina) does not return to the series, but coincidentally appears as Terri in the 2000 Disney TV movie *Phantom of the Megaplex*, another adaptation of Gaston Leroux's classic *The Phantom of the Opera*.

-Actor Philip Eddolls (Corey) returns to the series in season two's "Attack of the Jack-O-Lanterns", and later also appears in one episode of *Are You Afraid of the Dark?*

EP.8:
"Piano Lessons Can Be Murder"
Airdate: December 8, 1995
Written by: Charles Lazer
Directed by: William Fruet
Based on the Goosebumps book: Piano Lessons Can Be Murder (#13)

Guest Cast

Ben Cook	Barclay Hope
Carolyn Scott	Aron Tager

Favorite Line:
"I must have your beautiful hands!"
-Dr. Shreek

Synopsis
Piano lessons can indeed be murder at Dr. Shreek's music school, where young Jerry has just started taking classes, despite a green-faced ghost's ominous warnings.

Review
Jerry's new in town and moving into his new house when he finds a piano playing by itself in his basement. Now he's got a hell of an imagination, but he knows there's nothing make believe about that. Quickly forgetting about the strangeness, he heads outside to play catch with himself when he meets a girl and her guitar. She invites him to jam with her sometime and he rushes inside to demand piano lessons from his parents, because he's desperate to make friends and he believes this is the best way, or so I assume.

Anyway, obviously the piano lessons will be bad news, and we know that from the title. He meets Dr. Shreek, a flamboyant Santa Claus-type, who is head over heels for piano, and for Jerry's hands for that matter. He also meets Mr. Toggle, the maintenance man, who according to Dr. Shreek "can build anything", hinting at the twist to come. But that's not all! I forgot to mention the green-faced ghost woman who haunts Jerry's piano at home, and even possess him at one point while he's practicing. She was the one playing the piano in the beginning, and she warns him to stay away from the Shreek School because "It's Evil. Eviiillll!" His parents continue to not believe him, as is par for the course in these types of shows.

He decides to ignore the warning from the random green ghost and go back to the school, where Dr. Shreek attacks him, desperately in need of his beautiful hands. He runs into Mr. Toggle, who presses a button and shuts down Dr. Shreek. You see he was neither a doctor nor a human. He was a robot! Toggle is the real threat because he's the one who wants to chop off Jerry's so-called beautiful hands. Not to worry, because that random green ghost lady appears to save Jerry and we find out she knew Toggle; she's his old piano teacher, or at least I assume she is by what is said. Jerry escapes to play another day and Toggle is kept prisoner in his basement taking piano lessons from the green ghost lady for eternity.

This episode is an example of two many ingredients spoiling the soup. The plot of Dr. Shreek and the robot reveal were enough, but the addition of this random green ghost confuses matters and makes things seem too contrived. Why does the ghost appear to Jerry before he's even taken lessons, or shown any interest? What purpose does her possessing him serve? Maybe she uses his body to help her travel to Shreek's place, because she does pop out of his body at the end, but it isn't really explained, so again I am just assuming. Also, if Jerry had not met that girl, he wouldn't have even thought twice about piano lessons, or if the piano hadn't played by itself in the beginning, and he still met that girl, he wouldn't have thought about piano and he wouldn't be taking the lessons. There are just too many contrived moments that don't work in its favor, and that green ghost is the sour apple that spoils the bushel for me. However, the presence of Aron Tager as Dr. Shreek is very welcomed and his performance is a delight, elevating the episode as a whole.

Series Mythology

-This is director William Fruet's first of twenty-seven episodes he will helm, becoming the most prolific director of the *Goosebumps* TV series.

-Actor Ben Cook (Jerry), will basically become a regular around here. He will return to the series two more times (technically three), when we see him again in the season two two-parter "Welcome to Dead House" and season three's "Shocker on Shock Street."

-Actor Erica Luttrell (Kim) will return to the series in season two's "Attack of the Jack-O-Lanterns".

-The great character actor Aron Tager (Dr. Shreek) finally appears in *Goosebumps*, after his run of six episodes playing the beloved recurring character Dr. Vink on *Are You Afraid of the Dark?*

EP.9:

"Return of the Mummy"

Airdate: December 22, 1995

Written by: Charles Lazer

Directed by: John Bell

Based on the Goosebumps book: Return of the Mummy (#23)

Guest Cast

Daniel DeSanto   Annick Obonsawin
Elias Zarou   Afrah Gouda

Favorite Line:

"Great present, dad. A dead bug."

-Sari

Synopsis

A teenage boy visiting his uncle in Egypt unwittingly awakens the moldering mummy of Prince Khor-Ru.

Review

    This is a really solid episode. It's got an old-fashioned feeling and it's told straight out with no major zigs and zags. While light on scares, it is also noticeably light on feints and bluffs and red-herrings plot-wise, which I appreciate. The mummy doesn't make an appearance until the last four minutes of the episode, but the wonderful set design and the claustrophobic nature of the proceedings really gives the whole thing a dread-filled ambience and more than makes up for the lack of mummy action. There is a twist, but it works because it doesn't take the story in another direction, and it's in keeping with the plot we are following.

    Daniel DeSanto is great here as the comic relief, gee-golly-gosh clumsy kid, who awakens the mummy. He's got a likable, yet annoying persona that really works to sell the character. When the mummy rises and grabs his hand, his reaction is pure gold, but for some reason everyone else in the scene is just nonchalantly watching, like he just stubbed his toe or something. I'm not saying the other cast members weren't good, but without DeSanto this would have easily been a snooze.

The twist comes when the reporter, who is tagging along with their search for Prince Khor-Ru, turns out to be his immortal sister! She has lived as a scarab beetle inside an amber pendant for four thousand years, waiting for his tomb to be found so she can resurrect him and they can conquer the world together, or something along those lines. Sure, this is a hokey premise, but so are mummies. The twist works really well and doesn't just give us a left turn for shock's sake, but enriches the story, as a good twist is supposed to do. Remember when we found out Bruce Willis was a ghost in *The Sixth Sense?* What if in the last minute they had also revealed that the movie took place on Mars? See, what I mean? A twist is a powerful weapon and too many is too much.

Another thing I learned from this episode is that ancient Egyptian mummies speak perfect English. Who knew?

<u>Series Mythology</u>

-This episode is actually an adaptation of the sequel book *Return of the Mummy*, instead of the first Egyptian adventure with Gabe, *The Curse of the Mummy's Tomb*, and that's why the mummy returns, even though we never saw it before.

-Daniel DeSanto (Gabe) appears here after starring as Tucker, one of the recurring Midnight Society members in *Are You Afraid of the Dark?* His Egyptian adventure took place between the original cancelation of *Dark?*, and the revival in 1999, where he took the lead in the Midnight Society. DeSanto is the ONLY member of the Midnight Society to appear in the *Goosebumps* series.

-Annick Obonsawin (Sari) returns to the series in body only as the actor inside the Slappy costume for season two's "Night of the Living Dummy 3".

-Peter Jarvis, who walked like an Egyptian as Prince Khor-Ru, was apparently the go-to mummy guy because he will appear as another bandage-bedazzled dead guy in season two's "Don't Wake Mummy".

EP.10:
"Night of the Living Dummy 2"

<u>Airdate</u>: January 12, 1996

<u>Written by</u>: Rick Drew

<u>Directed by</u>: Ron Oliver

<u>Based on the Goosebumps book</u>: <u>Night of the Living Dummy 2</u> (#31)

Guest Cast

Maggie Castle	Caterina Scorsone
Andrew Sardella	Gina Clayton

<u>Favorite Line:</u>

"Hey Sara, wanna play?"

-Slappy

Synopsis

Amy's not into dolls, she's into dummies. Unluckily for her, her new one is really into her and wants to turn her into his slave. He walks, he talks, his name is Slappy, and he's no dummy!

Review

This is as tight and well paced as it gets when it comes to *Goosebumps*. Not only is it notable as the introduction of the series icon character, Slappy, but it's a perfect episode in terms of distilling a whole book into a half-hour show and making it feel like a fully fleshed out feature, instead of a short film. The work from writer Rick Drew and director Ron Oliver really delivers a satisfying sequence of events that always feel connected and never out-of-left-field, and the twist ending, if you can really call it that, makes sense and enriches what we previously thought we knew about the self-contained world of the episode.

Amy's dad finds Slappy in a second-hand store, just "sitting in the window". Now, since there is no first part, and we are basing our knowledge strictly on the TV adaptations, we have to assume Slappy has always been alive, or possessed by that green mist we see at the end. Perhaps he moves himself into that window seat to attract a potential buyer, which worked out for him.

  Amy's goofy puppet Dennis breaks apart, and her dad comes to the rescue with Slappy. Slappy instantly starts to make trouble, and here is where the episode starts to take a downturn, until Slappy reveals his master plan at the end. The downturn, for me, is that this is basically Chucky from the *Child's Play* franchise, but without the guts. In fact, Slappy even steals Chucky's famous catch phrase once. However, Slappy doesn't kill folks, he just paints stick figures on a painting and causes Amy to destroy her dad's guitar. You have to admit that these are pretty lame incidents, but when it's revealed that Slappy was trying to frame Amy and make her seem Looney Tunes in front of her family, then all the kiddie stuff makes sense. Also, I am aware this is a show for kids, and Slappy couldn't kill anyone, so the insanity route is almost the perfect crime for him and I applaud his escapades now.

  If you were trying to get some hooked on *Goosebumps*, or showcase a signature episode to some noob, then this would be the one. It feels like a movie, and that's best compliment one can give to an anthology show's stand-alone episode. Slappy, despite meeting an untimely crack-up thanks to Dennis, the OTHER living dummy, will return to fight another day.

<u>Series Mythology</u>

-Slappy's first appearance is an adaptation of the second book in the "dummy" series. The first one featured a different evil dummy, and that's probably why there isn't an adaptation for "Night of the Living Dummy"?

-Writer Rick Drew's first of ten episodes for the series.

-Ron Stefaniuk, creature creator and FX jack-of-all trades for the entire run of the series, steps into the limelight as the voice of Slappy. Cathal Dodd, however, steps into Slappy's voice for season two's "Night of the Living Dummy 3". Ron will return to voice the character in Slappy's third appearance, season three's "Bride of the Living Dummy". As a side note, Ron was later a puppeteer on the film *Bride of Chucky*, and no doubt leaned on his Slappy experience, since he also puppeteered our favorite wooden villain.

-Caterina Scorsone (Sara Kramer) will return for an epic three-parter in season three's "Chillogy".

-Richard Fitzpatrick (Mr. Kramer) will return in season four's two-parter "How I Got My Shrunken Head".

-Kerry Duff returns for the last time here, after appearing this season in "Welcome to Camp Nightmare". She will reunite with Shadia Simmons, who played her sister Alicia, to play sisters in "The Tale of the Night Nurse", the series finale of *Are You Afraid of the Dark?*

EP.11:
"My Hairiest Adventure"
Airdate: January 19, 1996
Written by: Michael Short
Directed by: David Warry-Smith
Based on the Goosebumps book: My Hairiest Adventure (#26)
Guest Cast:

Aaron Bartkiw	Courtney Greig
Ric Reid	Alison Hope

Favorite Line (there are so many in this one!):

"Are you growing some unexpected hair?"

-Lily

"Doesn't anybody shave in this house?"

-Larry

"Hairy Larry; hair on his head, hair on his mind."

-Lily

"It was pretty embarrassing talking to a girl about body hair."

-Larry

"Mom, dad, something weird's happening. I saw Lily. I think she's a dog!"

-Larry

Synopsis
Larry Boyd's got hair sprouting in new and interesting places. He isn't facing the typical teen issues of puberty, but something weird is dogging him.

Review
Not sure why, but this episode uses HEAVY amounts of voiceover; especially for stuff that the audience would already know, or is already being shown, and doesn't need to be told. That's one of the old adages of film: show, don't tell. This one does both, to a detriment, but I have to assume that they

believed their audience- children, in this case- would need their hand held for this particular story. Believe me, they don't.

Larry, called coincidentally enough "Hairy Larry" by his friends, finds some bottles of instant tan lotion in the garage while practicing with his... well, garage band. They all smear it on to make themselves look like "bronze gods" for their upcoming audition. Larry goes overboard with the stuff and this is where his situation gets a bit hairier. He starts to grow Wolfman levels of fuzz all over his arms and legs, and his friends, who also tried the lotion, start mysteriously disappearing, as well.

This episode is super-goofy, due to the overuse of voiceover and some of the acting choices made, but the plotting and twist are actually rather brilliant. Once Larry realizes all of his friends have turned into dogs, he himself devolves into a Golden Retriever (the same exact one from the *Goosebumps* opening credits, in a not-so-subtle meta-narrative move). We are lead to believe the sun tan lotion turned him from a human into a dog, and his parents are totally fine with this new arrangement. However, here comes the kicker, which is actually as brutal and tragic in its reality, as it is incredibly satisfying. It turns out that the town doc, Dr. Murkin, had found a way to turn dogs into humans, and that Larry was NEVER a human. He was always a dog, and now he is back to his "normal" self. This means, I deduce, that the creepy guy in his friend's closet, and the suntan lotion were just red herrings all along. Or maybe some of the expired chemicals in the lotion counter-acted the "dog-to-human" genetics. Now when Murkin showed up to inject Larry, I believe the parents had then decided to take his humanity away. It's horrifying, but it's a twist that expands the universe of the episode in meaningful ways. Poor Larry, stuck in the dog days of summer, for the rest of his life. Is he better off? No school, no bills, no worries? I'd choose Human, but that's just me. If I had always been a dog from the beginning, who knows? This episode vaguely reminds me of another Canadian oddity, the so-called children's film *The Peanut Butter Solution*. What's it about? You won't believe me, but here goes: a boy sneaks into an abandoned house where two old people ghosts scare him and he looses all his hair; then the ghosts follow him home and give him a magic recipe to grow his hair back which includes raw eggs and dead flies, and it works; long, lush, lustrous hair grows all over him and he is kidnapped by his art teacher, so he can shave the boy and use the newly-grown hair as bristles for his new line of paintbrushes. That's the plot. See, I told you you wouldn't believe me. Look it up, I'm not making any of that up. There's a reason I called it an oddity.

<u>Series Mythology</u>

-There seems to be some discrepancy as to this episode's order in the series. According to airdates, it's episode eleven, but some have it listed as episode thirteen, with the two-parter "Stay Out of the Basement" coming first. However, according to airdates, this episode showed first, so I am sticking with the airdate order.

-Director David Warry-Smith's first and only time helming an episode.

-Writer Michael Short's first and only time writing an episode.

-Suzanne Cyr (Mrs. Turnbull), Lily's mom, is the only actor to return to *Goosebumps,* in another "hair" related episode, for season two's "Bad Hare Day".

-The unassuming doctor that sets Larry on his hair-raising journey is named Murkin. The term "Merkin" stands for fake pubic hair. Coincidence? You decide.

EP.12:
"Stay Out of the Basement Pt.1"
Airdate: January 26, 1992
Written by: Sean Kelly
Directed by: William Fruet
Based on the Goosebumps book: Stay Out of the Basement (#2)

Guest Cast
Beki Lantos (as Rebecca Henderson)	Blake McGrath
Lucy Peacock	Judah Katz

Favorite Line:
"Stay out of the basement!"
-Dad

Synopsis
Margaret and Casey's dad is a botanist, and they've always been concerned about his obsession with his work, but due to the mysterious experiments he's been recently conducting in the basement, they're now concerned with their own safety.

Review
This is a genuinely terrifying two-parter. The house setting is drab and dreary, but it sets the stage for the menace to creep in. Margaret and Casey are a bit bland when it comes to character work, but they're supposed to stand in for every boy and girl watching the show, so it makes sense that they act more like avatars than their own individual selves. We've all worried about something mysterious in our neighborhood or what-have-you, and when it happens at home, it's even more of a sinister situation.

The first-part manages to deliver some great creepy moments, easing us into it like a horror film should, feeding us a few tantalizing nuggets, but never spoiling our appetite. In one scene, dad sits the kids down to explain what he's doing. He says sometimes botanists cross-breed plants, but that's not what he's doing. A half a dozen scenes later he finally spills the beans, when he isn't really himself anymore, and reveals that he is trying to make a plant that is part animal, because who wouldn't want that. It's some kind of an answer to the goings-on, but not really, and that bit of info keeps us hooked. Throughout the first-half we watch a plant attacking Margaret, we see dad bleeding chlorophyll with plants growing out of the top of his head, and we've pretty much deduced that dad's got more than a green thumb in the garden. These moments are blatantly weird, but vague enough to keeps us wondering. The standout here is Judah Katz (Dr. Brewer) as the intense, fixated scientist dad. The stone-faced looks and the creepiness of his performance really help to sell the importance of staying out of the darn basement. His subtle performance showcases range and really makes the dad not just a tyrannical father figure, but also a mysterious force to be reckoned with, and that reckoning will come with our next episode!

Series Mythology

-Writer Sean Kelly will only write the "Stay Out of the Basement" two-parter and never cross paths with *Goosebumps* again.

-The "video game" Casey is playing is pixilated footage from the episode "Welcome to Camp Nightmare". This is the first time an episode references another episode in an indirect way so, if you really think about it, that means that none of these *Goosebumps* stories exist in the same universe.

EP.13:
"Stay Out of the Basement Pt.2"
Airdate: January 26, 1992
Written by: Sean Kelly
Directed by: William Fruet
Based on the Goosebumps book: Stay Out of the Basement (#2)

Guest Cast

Beki Lantos (as Rebecca Henderson)   Blake McGrath
Lucy Peacock   Judah Katz

Favorite Line:
"You're not a mad scientist, are you, dad?"
-Casey

Synopsis
Margaret and Casey have had enough and they want to get to the bottom of all of this, but that bottom lies in the forbidden basement, where they come face to face with the horrible truth.

Review
This second-half isn't as well paced as the first one, but it certainly isn't boring, either. It hits the ground running with a bit of snooping on the kids' parts, but when their efforts are frustrated they decide to head right to the source for the truth. As Margaret says, "the truth is in the basement", so they grab some weed killer and a crowbar and raid the basement jungle. The majority of the episode takes place here as they brave the elements and discover their dad, or a copy of their dad, tied up in a closet. He claims to be their real pops, but when the other one in the baseball cap shows up he explains that the one in the closet is a plant-based copy. Now the kids must decide which father to spray with weed killer. If it were up to me I'd spray both, because the human one wouldn't be harmed in the least and the plant one would die, but when their real dad (closet dad) calls Margaret by her

pet name, she knows baseball cap dad is the veggie, and she saves the day by melting him into mushy, creamed spinach.

I think this two-parter could have easily been one episode, because the halves here play lopsided in terms of pacing. If the inciting incident to finish this off was Margaret just deciding randomly to head back into the basement to look for answers, that could have come at any time after some of the weird moments of the first part. So for me, they don't work separately, in case you watched them out of order. As one whole chunk, it works fairly well pacing wise, but the ending is a bit rushed.

A highlight here is the creepy as hell basement jungle with faces melted into the trees and hand-plants grasping at our heroes. The last-second *Goosebumps* twist is also really horrifying when Margaret bends down to tie her shows and all the red flowers around her start calling out to her, claiming they're all REALLY her dad. The implications of that are almost too heavy for a simple kids show, so kudos for the team behind the series for keeping that intact from the book.

<u>Series Mythology</u>

-Actor Beki Lantos (Margaret) will return to the series in season four's "How I Got My Shrunken Head".

-Actor Lucy Peacock, who played Margaret's mom, will return in an uncredited role as a teacher in season two's "You Can't Scare Me!"

EP.14:

"It Came from Beneath the Sink"

<u>Airdate</u>: February 2, 1996

<u>Written by</u>: Rick Drew

<u>Directed by</u>: David Winning

<u>Based on the Goosebumps book</u>: <u>It Came from Beneath the Sink!</u> (#30)

<u>Guest Cast</u>

Katharine Isabelle	Tyrone Savage
Amanda Tapping	Howard Hoover

<u>Favorite Line:</u>

"This is better than the X-Files."

-Carlo

<u>Synopsis</u>

A girl discovers a living, telekinetic sponge monster in her new home and that's just the start of her bad luck.

<u>Review</u>

Kat and her brother Daniel move into a new house, which is only eight minutes and forty-six seconds away from her old home by bicycle, and discover a Grool living under the kitchen sink. What's a Grool? Come on, people! Everyone knows "a Grool is mythical creature, believed to be a living bad luck charm", as Kat and Daniel's pal Carlo (an X-Files fan, I might add) states in the episode. Grool also feeds on the bad luck it causes, so it's really just a vicious cycle kind of monster, and that's no fun for anyone. The good news is they didn't find a Lanx, which is a vampire potato that feeds on your life force.

No one believes Kat at first, until the sponge reveals itself to Daniel and Carlo as well, and they have to team up to either dispose of the creature, or donate it to science. It may have also killed their dog, coincidentally named Killer, and no one really wants that goofy sponge creature around. Kat leaves it with her science teacher, but that may spell her doom, so they return late at night to retrieve it, only to find themselves in a battle of good intentions with the Grool, where the strongest weapon against it may be compliments. Why fight fire with fire, when you can kill it with kindness? Of course, this wouldn't be *Goosebumps* without a twisty, unhappy ending, so worry not, friend, because we'll get to meet a Lanx before the credits role!

This episode feels the most well-paced like a tightly-contained mini-movie than other episodes, and speaks to the viability of keeping the stories in one-off chunks, instead of the two-parters, which so far play uneven. The cast is really good here, especially young Katharine Isabelle (Kat), who would go on to make quite a name for herself in horror movies. The writing from Rick Drew is tight, as we saw with his first episode "Night of the Living Dummy 2", and the directing from series newcomer David Winning is smooth and on-point.

The one draw back here is just how goofy the Grool looks. It's basically a natural sea sponge with glowing dots for eyes and a small mouth crammed with jagged teeth that prevent it to barely open its mouth and eat anything, but since it doesn't feed on meat, only bad luck, I guess it doesn't need to open its jaws that wide… or need teeth for that matter, actually. Anyway, every time they cut to it you can't help but laugh, or at least smirk at it. However, maybe that was the idea. Maybe here we see that anything, even a common household item, is something to be wary of, and that is in essence what *Goosebumps* is all about. The supernatural, the weird, the strange, the otherworldly, is all around us, and even if you're careful, you'll probably bump into it eventually.

Series Mythology

-Director David Winning's first and only episode for *Goosebumps*, although previously he had helmed ten episodes of *Are You Afraid of the Dark?*

-Actor Tyrone Savage (Daniel) not only has a great name, but also will return to the series in the season three episode: "Strained Peas".

-Amanda Tapping (Mom) does not return to the series, but went on to have a huge career in TV, which included the full ten-season run on *Stargate SG-1*.

-A couple more meta-*Goosebumps* moments take place in this episode. There is another appearance from Sabre the "werewolf" from "Welcome to Camp Nightmare", when Daniel and Carlo are watching TV, and a remix of the theme song is used at the end to soothe the savage beast that is the Grool. I assume the former is because "Camp Nightmare" was one of the first filmed and they had that footage available and needed something for the TV, so they sampled themselves once more. Does this mean this takes place in the same universe as "Stay Out of the Basement"? We may never know.

EP.15:
"Say Cheese and Die"
Airdate: February 9, 1996
Written by: Bruce Edwards
Directed by: Ron Oliver
Based on the Goosebumps book: Say Cheese and Die (#4)

Guest Cast

Ryan Gosling	Akiva David
Renessa Blitz	Caley Wilson

Favorite Line:
"Say Cheese!"
-Greg

Synopsis
Greg and his pals find a mysterious camera that seemingly predicts the future with every snap, and the future isn't looking bright.

Review
This is one of the first in the series that I consider sci-fi instead of horror. Technology-run-amok is one of the staples of science fiction, and here we have the perfect engine for said "amok"-ness. The camera, something you'd see in *Star Wars*, is at the center of the shenanigans here, and Spidey the mysterious hobo mentions that it predicts the future. However, if Greg was able to change things and bring back Shari by tearing up her picture, then wouldn't that negate its future-prediction powers? I believe the camera is like the Grool in the last episode, and that whatever you take a pic of is cursed with bad luck, so that's why the photos are never the person covered in jewels or what-have-you. It may predict a possible future, but that future leans toward the wrong side of the tracks as far as luck is concerned, in my opinion. Breezily directed by Ron Oliver and with a fast-paced script from Bruce Edwards, this one plays almost like a *Twilight Zone* episode more than a typical *Goosebumps*, and that's not a bad thing. The kid cast grounds it in

reality, as far as *Goosebumps* is concerned, and the standout here is our lead Greg, played by future Hollywood movie star Ryan Gosling, who's friendship with director Ron Oliver saw him also appear in one of Ron's episodes for *Are You Afraid of the Dark?*

The one element here that isn't addressed in detail is the character of Spidey. The name alone is questionable, because he's not a spider (what a twist that would have been!), but his existence as a hobo in a warehouse full of strange gadgets is never explained, and in a way I appreciate that, but I just wish the character had returned to do more, or give us more, but ultimately that was up to Mister Stine. We do know from the book that his real name is Dr. Fritz Fredericks and that he died of fright in the book when his picture was taken by Shari. In the show he was trapped by the camera, and then subsequently released, so technically he's still out there… somewhere.

<u>Series Mythology</u>

-Writer Bruce Edwards' final episode for *Goosebumps.*

-Actor Richard McMillan (Spidey) not only returns to *Goosebumps* in the season three episode "Teacher's Pet", but coincidentally enough he starred as the photographer with the mysterious camera in the *Are You Afraid of the Dark?* episode: "The Tale of the Curious Camera", which also starred Christian Tessier (Mickey Ward) and was directed by Ron Oliver! Was Ron planning a secret, alternate reality sequel? The magic eight ball points to yes, as far as I'm concerned.

-Actor Scott Speedman (Officer Madison) cameos here under huge, mirrored sunglasses, but would go on to a bigger Hollywood career, including the full four-season run on the beloved series *Felicity*.

-During Greg's dream sequence, this episode's famous *Goosebumps* book cover of the skeletons at the barbeque is faithfully reproduced.

-When we meet the bullies, Greg called them "Joey Ferris and Mickey Knox", but the character of Mickey is credited as Mickey Ward, as it originally appears in the book. Was this a goof? A typo? Magic eight ball has no answers for this one.

-There is a sequel to this episode in season three titled "Say Cheese and Die… Again". Ron Oliver returns to direct, and the characters return, but the parts are all completely recast. Spidey only appears in flashbacks, as well.

EP.16:
"A Night in Terror Tower Pt.1"
Airdate: February 25, 1996
Written by: Dan Angel & Billy Brown
Directed by: William Fruet
Based on the Goosebumps book: A Night in Terror Tower (#27)

Guest Cast

Kathryn Short	Corey Sevier
Robert Collins	Diego Matamoros

Favorite Line:
"Lovely postcards depicting the instruments of torture are available in the gift shop."
-Tour Guide

Synopsis
Siblings Sue and Eddie slip into a time warp while touring London's famous Terror Tower and find their very existence threatened.

Review
Not a ton of scary stuff happens in this first-half. Like most of the two-parters the first portion is all set up, like a protracted first act. The bulk of the episode is devoted to the tour of the Terror Tower itself with the tour guide calling his customers "tourists", but it sounds like a racial slur the way he says it. I've taken tons of tours, and none of the guides have called me a tourist, which is what I am, but usually the guides want us to feel included, and pointing out that we are all just passing through makes it feel very elitist. Small point, but it niggled at me, and this is where I get to express those niggles.

The rest of the episode consists of Sue and Eddie running away from one of the wax figures, who has sprung to life, or so we are led to believe, and wants to drag them into the dungeon. They escape, thanks to the help of a flurry of CG bats, and find that their memories are scrambled. They remember the hotel they're staying at, and the room number, but forget their last names. The episode ends with Sue turning to her brother and stating that something is wrong, and I agree with her. There is plenty wrong.

This two-parter has more holes than a block of Swiss cheese, but we will get into it better when we have all the ingredients to mix into the pot next episode. I do want you to remember a few things: they have American accents (ok Canadian, but North American, basically), they don't understand the British pound monetary system, they know of a hotel that did not exist during the operating years of the Terror Tower, they are wearing modern-day clothing, and they know the term "conference" as a definition for a gathering of people. To properly unpack this tale, we will need to absorb the events of part two, so onward we go!

Series Mythology

-Kathryn Short (Sue) returns to the series after helping out Carly Beth with "The Haunted Mask", and we shall see her again when she reunites with both of those in season two's "The Haunted Mask 2".

-In reality, there is no Terror Tower, but it is a reference to the Tower of London, a famous tourist spot and former torture dungeon. The series, filmed in Canada, needed a stand-in for the tower, so this two-parter was filmed at the Casa Loma Castle in Toronto, which does not date back to the middle ages, but the early 1900s.

EP.17:
"A Night in Terror Tower Pt.2"
<u>Airdate:</u> February 25, 1996
<u>Written by:</u> Dan Angel & Billy Brown
<u>Directed by:</u> William Fruet
<u>Based on the Goosebumps book:</u> <u>A Night in Terror Tower</u> (#27)

Guest Cast

Kathryn Short   Corey Sevier
Robert Collins   Diego Matamoros

Favorite Line:
"Is this a theme park?
-Sue

Synopsis
Sue and Eddie are caught and transported back in time to the Terror Tower's heyday, where they face a shocking truth and an executioner's sharpened axe.

Review

    This is the least sensible story in the *Goosebumps* series, as far as I'm concerned, and by far the least goose bump inducing. When something doesn't add up, none of it adds up. I can suspend disbelief, and allow magical leeway only so far before it all gets too ridiculous.

    Sue and Eddie are captured by the man in black at their hotel and are pulled back through time to the middle ages. Morgred, the King's sorcerer, reveals that Sue and Eddie are actually Susanna and Edward, the princess and prince of York. He used three white stones to cast a spell and send them into the future to prevent their beheading at the hands of their wicked uncle, who murdered their parents, the King and Queen. Once the spell has worn off, their American accents disappear and they switch to English accents, and the modern-day clothes vanish into royal finery. They are scheduled for execution at the hands of their uncle, but Eddie, or I should say Prince Edward, uses his previously established pickpocket skills to steal back the three white stones and return them to Morgred to allow them to return to the future. Morgred ends up traveling back with them and the kids are American again with modern clothes, except Morgred hangs on to his English accent for some reason, and viola, a happy ending for once.

So now that we have all the pieces, lets try to make this puzzle look like the one on the box. If a magic spell managed to send two kids into the future, how could it also give them American accents, give them modern clothing, give them knowledge of modern day locations (the hotel) and terms (the conference) and events (the tour), and wipe their memories completely at the same time? And don't say "magic", because that's just cheating, and frankly bad writing. Their accents and clothing should have vanished the moment they were returned to the past, and not only when they were reminded of who they were. With this massive reveal-bomb dropped on the plot, the first-half of this two-parter plays even worse, because all that makes less sense now.

The more I look at it, the less any of these pieces fit together, and I'll be darned if I want to spend too much time with this puzzle, because I have a feeling it's missing a few necessary corners.

Despite the ridiculous plot, the art directing and set design is ridiculously on point and are the standout elements of this second-half. You can tell they spent their money to make you believe you were in a weathered, old-fashioned portion of London, and their budget for extras was probably tripled, too. Every Brit in Canada was no doubt called in for this one, and I for one appreciate that effort, even if the bones of the piece are brittle.

<u>Series Mythology</u>

-Corey Sevier (Eddie) will return to the series for another two-parter titled "The Cry of the Cat" in season four.

-Diego Matamoros (Morgred) will return as the voice of the Shadow Figure in season four's two-parter "The Ghost Next Door".

-Sophie Bennett (Unnamed Medieval Girl) will return with a bigger role in season three's "The Bride of the Living Dummy".

-R.L. Stine appears to intro and outro the episode, like Rod Serling, from inside a dungeon's souvenir shop.

EP.18:
"The Werewolf of Fever Swamp Pt.1"
Airdate: May 17, 1996
Written by: Neal Shusterman
Directed by: William Fruet
Based on the Goosebumps book: The Werewolf of Fever Swamp (#14)

Guest Cast

Brendan Fletcher   Maria Ricossa
Mairon Bennett   Geoffrey Bowes

Favorite Line:
"Is this a bloodstain?"
-Grady

Synopsis
Grady and his family move into a new home inside a swamp and he soon discovers that one of his neighbors might just be a werewolf.

Review

A classic monster in a new, fresh setting is always a cause for excitement, but unfortunately this first-half is really kind of a snooze. No werewolf appearance whatsoever and only a brief tease with some howling. Toss in an obvious red herring in the form of a swamp hermit and a random, stray dog jump scare, and it still amounts to very little. I realize that most of these two-parters are using the first-half for set up, but "Welcome to Camp Nightmare" and "The Haunted Mask", just to name a few, weren't afraid to hit the ground running with their first installment.

The cast is serviceable here, and Brendan Fletcher as Grady is likable enough to want us to tag along with his adventures. His adventures include helping his parents with their experiment where they plan to let loose a group of deer to see if they thrive in the swamp, and if that isn't the worse reason to relocate to the swamps, I don't know what is. And why does almost every episode of *Goosebumps* have to revolve around some kid moving into a new house. We're at the end of season one here with this two-parter and this is the third kid-moving-in plot we've had!

Not much more can be said about this one. We meet all the pieces on the chessboard and, knowing how *Goosebumps* works, we already know how they're going to move. The swamp hermit will not be a werewolf, but most likely a werewolf hunter looking for revenge or something. Will Blake, the friendly next-door neighbor kid, will be the surprise werewolf and Grady will have to kill his new friend before he ends up like hamburger helper. His newly adopted dog, which literally came out of nowhere, will save the day and push the werewolf into the bog we saw Grady almost drown in. Am I right? Let's head into the next episode and finish off this first season with a howl.

Series Mythology

-We get another fun meta wink when we find the haunted mask image from the cover of the *Goosebumps* book slapped onto the bottom of Grady's skateboard.

EP.19:
"The Werewolf of Fever Swamp Pt.2"
Airdate: May 17, 1996
Written by: Neal Shusterman
Directed by: William Fruet
Based on the Goosebumps book: The Werewolf of Fever Swamp (#14)

Guest Cast

Brendan Fletcher	Maria Ricossa
Mairon Bennett	Geoffrey Bowes

Favorite Line:
"Got him!"
-Swamp Hermit

Synopsis
Grady and his family finally come face to face with the Fever Swamp Werewolf and his ferocious appetite.

Review
    Well, I was right. Everything I had predicted in the previous episode came true. The *Goosebumps* formula is becoming too transparent, but I'm sure the young audience probably didn't connect all the dots. Again, we have a long stretch of nothing happening, which I think is supposed to equate to suspense, but it doesn't really work here. We do, however, finally get to see the werewolf and it's a pretty good full body suite with a gnarly face. It goes baboon-crazy on the barn where Grady's mom and sister are hiding in, and then it goes after Grady.

    Thanks to a lunar eclipse, the transformation wears off enough for Grady to realize that it's his new friend Will under all that hair, and then the moon returns and so does the full wolf, but never fear because Vandal, his newly acquired pet, body slams the werewolf down a hill and into, you guessed it, the deep quicksand bog that nearly claimed Grady last time. The twist here is that apparently Grady did not escape unscathed and the episode ends with him howling at the moon. Is he infected? Does he have swamp fever? I choose booth.

This episode reminded me of the Dean Koontz movie and book *Watchers*, where a similar dog protects humans from a werewolf/bigfoot type monster; that was a fantastic story, this one is ok. I think the directing and scenery were great, and a welcomed change to the Canadian suburbs we've been living in for the past whole season, but the slow pace and holding back on the werewolf reveal really did take the bite out of this one for me.

Series Mythology

-Writer Neal Shusterman's first of seven scripts for the series. He will next write season two's "Night of the Living Dummy 3".

SEASON TWO
Original airdate:
August 10, 1996 - July 20, 1997

EP.20:
"Be Careful What You Wish for"

<u>Airdate</u>: August 10, 1996

<u>Written by:</u> Charles Lazer

<u>Directed by:</u> René Bonniére

<u>Based on the Goosebumps book</u>: Be Careful What You Wish for... (#12)

Guest Cast

Melody Johnson	Ellen-Ray Hennessy
Susan Cooke	Robin Weekes

Favorite Line:
"Wanna help me strangle Judith?"

-Samantha

Synopsis

Clumsy Samantha meets a fairy Godmother, but she'll find out that getting her wishes to come true may be the unluckiest thing to have happened to her yet.

Review

Season two kicks off with a fast-paced episode that uses its time wisely and is the most bird-themed episode of the series. Maybe Mr. Stine's family had just gotten a parrot, or maybe he was just really into feathers while writing the book this episode is based on, but it is very hard to not notice the blatant connections to the avian world. The problem is that if there's a deeper, mythical meaning, it is lost on me. So we'll chalk it up to coincidence.

Samantha BYRD, school klutz, is only on the basketball team because she's tall, not because she's super amazing at slamming hoops. Frustrated and disheartened by the jerky girls at her school, most notably her main tormentor Judith, she prepares to drag her feet through the rest of her life until she meets a flamboyant lady in old-fashioned dress, dripping in FEATHERS. Her name is Clarissa, and she is obviously a raven, or a crow, or... look, basically she's a BIRD, and that's my point. Now here is where

Clarissa explains it all (heh heh): she will grant Sam three wishes and hopes it will better her situation. Of course, this is *Goosebumps* so the wishes will not be exactly what she asked for.

Her first wish is to be the best player on her team, and the next day during a game her entire team is struck down by the flu or something and by default she is the best player. Her next wish, and my favorite, is to be left alone by everyone. She wishes that everyone would just buzz off, and not only do all the kids in her school turn into flies, but the entire world along with them. Despite some wonky slow-mo shots, this is the standout portion of the episode because it gives the story and the world itself a grander scope. Plus, wrangling all those flies must have been a pain in the behind, so I admire the production's dedication. Her third wish undoes the fly problem and turns her nemesis Judith into her best friend, but to an obsessive level. Judith's stalker habits are the straw that breaks Sam's back, but Clarissa gives her an easy out with one more wish.   In a gruesome, technically happy twist, Sam wishes for Judith to have met Clarissa and not herself. Giving someone like Judith this incredible power doesn't sound like a great idea, but Sam knows Judith will use it selfishly, and it pays off accordingly. Judith wishes to be admired by all, and Clarissa turns her into a statue. The last shot is of Clarissa in her bird form perching on Judith's newly cemented head and readying herself for a good bird poo.

Essentially, our sad sack heroine just turned into a murderer. Indirectly she caused not only the death of Judith, but erased her from existence, because Judith cannot wish herself out of the statue. It's something a kid probably wouldn't notice, but if you really think about it this ending is quite tragic and jaw-droppingly sad. Has Sam bettered her situation? Yes, in a sense, but she is no longer the innocent she was at the beginning, and that's truly horrifying, despite the big smile on Sam's face at the end.

Series Mythology

-Director René Bonniére's first of two episodes for the series. He will return later this season for "You Can't Scare Me!"

-Actor Robin Weekes (Cory) will return, coincidentally, in season three's "The House of No Return".

-Montrose Middle School is actually John English Junior Middle School in Etobicoke, Toronto, Ontario.

EP.21:
"Attack of the Mutant Pt. 1"

<u>Airdate</u>: September 7, 1996
<u>Written by</u>: Dan Angel & Billy Brown
<u>Directed by</u>: William Fruet
<u>Based on the Goosebumps book</u>: Attack of the Mutant (#25)

<u>Guest Cast</u>

Dan Warry-Smith	Melissa Bathory
Maurice Godin	Mag Ruffman

<u>Favorite Line:</u>
"Wanna trade?"
-Wilson

Synopsis

Comic book fan Skipper is shocked to discover that the villain from his favorite comic book has popped out of the panels and into reality.

Review

Our hero, Skipper, does not only have a horribly embarrassing first name, but is your basic comic book nerd; the kind who will grow up and complain about the costume inaccuracies in the latest super hero movie. Of course, he has to grow up first, and his favorite comic character may actually be the one to prevent him from doing so.

This has got to be my favorite two-parter in the series. It's not very scary in the *Goosebumps* senses, but it's clever, and refreshing, and the writing by series stalwarts Dan Angel and Billy Brown is hilarious and feels authentic to kid-speak. There is a great moment where Skipper and his pal Wilson both have tuna sandwiches and they decide to trade sandwiches anyway. It's a little random thing, but it feels natural, like something kids would do in real life, and it makes the characters shines because they aren't just spouting exposition or set-up. As a viewer I appreciate these little touches of effortless humanity that make the scene and the players within seem more lifelike and less like puppets going through the motions.

The first-half of the two-parter establishes Skipper and his obsession and sets up a premise where a comic book villain, in this case the Masked Mutant, has found a way to transfer into the real world. The first-half of this episode feels meaty and engrossing, but the second-half sadly devolves into Skipper and his new friend Libby, who loves to over-pronounce her words, just wandering around a set, thereby losing its momentum. The green screen work in those scenes is really wonky, but the sets look pretty decent; reminding me of the inside of the clown spaceship in *Killer Klowns from Outer Space*. The episode ends with Skipper coming face to face with the Masked Mutant. Is it curtains for our hero? We'll find out in the next thriller installment of *Skipper Vs. The Masked Mutant...* I mean, *Goosebumps*.

Series Mythology

-I couldn't find any info on this, but I'll bet that actor Dan Warry-Smith (Skipper) is related to the director of "My Hairiest Adventure", David Warry-Smith.

-Look closely and you'll see some conspicuous advertising for *Goosebumps* on the side of a bus, giving it a resounding two thumbs up.

EP.22:
"Attack of the Mutant Pt. 2"

<u>Airdate</u>: September 7, 1996
<u>Written by</u>: Dan Angel & Billy Brown
<u>Directed by</u>: William Fruet
<u>Based on the Goosebumps book</u>: Attack of the Mutant (#25)

Guest Cast

Dan Warry-Smith	Melissa Bathory
Maurice Godin	Mag Ruffman

Favorite Line:
"You know, kid, if you're gonna be a superhero, you've gotta start working out."

-The Galloping Gazelle

Synopsis
Skipper teams up with his favorite hero, the Galloping Gazelle, to defeat the morphing Masked Mutant before he rubs them both out of existence.

Review
Skipper puts his nerd skills to good use here in the ultimate nerd-fantasy, meta-take on fandom. After surviving his first foray in the Mutant's lair, he returns home to find the world around him warping into a comic book. When he receives a new issue of the Mutant's comic, he discovers himself in the pages with the heroic Galloping Gazelle trapped and at the mercy of the Mutant. Good ol' Skip decides to return to the Mutant's headquarters, finds the Galloping Gazelle, and frees him. Teaming up, they head deeper into the factory-like environment to save the day. Everything the Galloping Gazelle says is comedy gold, with Adam West basically playing his sixties Batman persona.

When the Masked Mutant arrives, the showdown begins. However, he really doesn't look like a villain. His bright colors and muscle suit make him look more like a hero than anything else; even the name doesn't give off bad guy vibes. Nevertheless, he's the heavy, and he proves too much for Gazelle, who takes off and leaves poor Skipper to face him alone. Libby shows up, but is revealed to be the Mutant in disguise. Why he would choose to pretend to be an underage girl, and for what purpose, is anyone's guess. The overwrought finale, filled with dangling threats, smoke, flashing sparks, and double-crosses, plays like the final act in a big budget superhero movie, hitting all the beats in a satisfying way. The twist here is that the Masked Mutant turned Skipper into a comic book character, then Skipper decided he was the Colossal Elastic Boy. Using his knowledge of the Elastic Boy's weaknesses and the Masked Mutant's weaknesses, he handily defeats the villain.

The unsung hero here is Skipper's mom, played by Mag Ruffman, who deftly handles her wayward son and her controlling husband in a Donna Reed sort of way, adding a fifties feel to the proceedings. In the last moments of the episode, she discovers ink on Skipper's hands and proceeds to scrub at it and wash it. If I had written this story, it would have ended with Skipper's mom washing away the ink, but accidentally washing Skipper away with it, since he had now become a real comic book character. It wouldn't have been a happy ending, but it would have been poetic; still, the ending where Skipper becomes a real super hero and may not need to escape into comic books, because he lives one now, is still highly rewarding.

<u>Series Mythology</u>

-Actor Dan Warry-Smith (Skipper) will return in the season three episode "Click".

-Actor Scott Wickware plays the Masked Mutant here, but will return later this season to play the man under another mask in "The Haunted Mask 2", and a guy in a hard hat for the two-parter "Welcome to Dead House".

-Legendary actor Adam West (The Galloping Gazelle) appeared in the first part in voice only, but this time he's in the flesh as the Masked Mutant's hostage. Just in case you don't know who he is, Mister West played a groovy version of the Dark Knight in the popular sixties TV series *Batman*.

EP.23:

"Bad Hare Day"

Airdate: September 14, 1996
Written by: Charles Lazer
Directed by: John Bell
Based on the Goosebumps book: Bad Hare Day (#41)

Guest Cast

Dov Tiefenbach	Robert Hamilton
Harvey Atkin	Tabitha Lupien

Favorite Line:
"What, and quit show business?"
-Tim

Synopsis

Tim Swanson wants to be a famous magician one day, and when he meets a talking rabbit with plans to steal a magic wand, he may have just found his way into showbiz.

Review

This is the strangest episode yet, and that's not necessarily a bad thing; it really depends on what you're looking for when you watch *Goosebumps*. This episode can be equally considered a goofy disappointment, or subtly brilliant. Where do I lean? I'm in the latter camp, because I consider this out-of-the-box (pun intended) tale to be really quite ingenious in its construction and that last second payoff turns what could have been a tragic ending into a happy one with some really heavy connotations. The reason some would lean in the other direction is that the episode plays a bit sloppy with its pacing and it isn't scary whatsoever. The story keeps shifting and the plot doesn't really develop until the end of the episode. We don't even meet our villain, El Sydney the rabbit, until the halfway point.

Examining the meat of the episode, these flaws are part of the fabric that makes this episode stand out from the standard *Goosebumps* episode. I appreciate the ditching of the formulaic elements and giving us a shifting storyline with a twist that is not only germane to the plot, but also legitimately satisfying. The young Dov Tiefenbach, as Tim, is a great lead and holds the episode together nicely, but the star is David Ferry as El Sydney's voice and then his human form.

This episode is an outlier in the series, but by being so it breaks new ground.

<u>Series Mythology</u>

-Actor Dov Tiefenbach (Tim) returns to the series in the season four two-parter "The Ghost Next Door".

-Actor Tabitha Lupien (Ginny) returns to the series in season three's "Click."

-Actor Suzanne Cyr, from "My Hairiest Adventure", is listed as Tim's Mom, but she does not appear in the episode, so I assume she was cut in the edit.

-Comedian Colin Mochrie cameos as a stone-faced stagehand, rescuing Tim from the locked room.

-There's a fun reference to Señor Wences, the famous ventriloquist, whose best known bit would include a final dialog with his puppet where he would ask the puppet in the box if it was "all right" and the puppet would seemingly respond from inside "S'alright", and El Sydney himself drops that nugget for those paying attention.

EP.24:

"The Headless Ghost"

<u>Airdate</u>: September 21, 1996
<u>Written by</u>: Dan Angel & Billy Brown
<u>Directed by</u>: Brian R.R. Hebb
<u>Based on the Goosebumps book</u>: The Headless Ghost (#37)

Guest Cast

Andreanne Benidir   Kenny Vadas
Dennis O'Connor   Sean Ryan

Favorite Line:

"Don't play innocent with me, girlie girl, or you'll find out that my bite is worse than my bark!"

-Andrew

Synopsis

Friends Duane and Stephanie don't believe Hill House, their local haunted house, is really full of ghosts at all until a mysterious boy helps them break in one night and they uncover the truth.

Review

This episode has the same problem that a future episode will have. That future episode is "Ghost Beach", and the problem there is that when the main kids go looking for a ghost, logic is thrown out the window and almost everyone turns out to be a ghost just because *Goosebumps* needs that twist ending. Here, it's the same darn thing, and it turns what could have been a very eerie episode into a major eye-roller. This is a case of the twist being more important than the story, and everything implodes because of it.

Side note, Duane and Stephanie call themselves the Terror Twins, and I thought I they were siblings, but according to multiple sources they have different last names, so the twin phrasing is weird. Let's look beyond that, however, to what this episode is really telling them (and us by default): Otto, the sea captain ghost, can somehow appear solid and interact with humans as another regular human, and when he wants to he can shut off his human side and turn into a ghost. Say what? Also, the ice cream fiend Seth can appear solid and then shift to ghost form, but the headless ghost kid is all ghost, all the time? Granted, none of us know the rules of the ghost world, and there is something to be said in favor of the author making his own rules as he goes along, but when it comes to ghosts interacting with solid matter and being basically skin and bones, I have to draw a line with my suspension of disbelief, and I believe even kids would be left confused by this episode. Throw in a last minute painting plot point and this thing becomes very hard to swallow, even for a *Goosebumps* episode.

Also, the Headless Ghost is barely in this, and I'm not sure why he's the star, because he has the least impact on the plot here. That plot isn't helped any by its slow build up and rushed and bewildering finale. It left me with so many questions, but it also left me with a sense of not caring, and that's because it played too goofy and broad, and ultimately I don't really need answers, I just need to not watch this one again. I will say that first-time director Brian R.R. Hebb does a great job with the material he was given.

Series Mythology

-The first and only episode directed by series cinematographer, Brian R.R. Hebb, who will wind up photographing 32 of the *Goosebumps* episodes.

-Actor Andreanne Benidir (Stephanie) will return in season three's "Bride of the Living Dummy".

-The use of the name Hill House is most likely a reference to the famed haunted house in the novel <u>The Haunting of Hill House</u> by Shirley Jackson, which has been adapted into two movies, and with a new TV show version in the works.

EP.25:
"Go Eat Worms"

<u>Airdate:</u> September 28, 1996
<u>Written by:</u> Rick Drew
<u>Directed by:</u> Steve DiMarco

Guest Cast

Noah Shebib	Kristin Fairlie
Caroline Yeager	Andre Ottley-Lorant

Favorite Line:

"Worms on the brain! Worms on the brain!"
-Regina & Beth (in sing-song)

Synopsis

Todd and his pal Danny are prepping their science fair experiment on worms, but what they don't know is that the night crawlers might have a few objections to it.

Review

This is by far the worst episode of the series. It's not scary, it makes no sense, and there is no real concrete plot. I could go on and on, but I think you get the drift.

Todd is obsessed with worms, and not in a teen idol way, but in a Jeffrey Dahmer kind of way. Not only is he breeding thousands of them for a so-called science fair project, but he's also gone to great lengths to cover his room in pictures and models of worms much like a serial killer would decorate their kill room with pictures of their victims. If that weren't bad enough, apparently he tortures the little slimy things, and they've had enough. I would have bought a story about sentient worms getting revenge on some jerky kid who was messing with them, but not only does a threat never really materialize, the worm story is abandoned halfway through after he learned his lesson by falling into a cave and fighting off a giant, goofy worm.

The worm payoff is set aside so we can have a joke twist, where he decides to do his project on fish, and for some reason the fish hate his guts so much that they drag him into the river presumably to kill him. Does this mean every animal in the world can sense the weirdo vibes coming off of this kid? I know I'm nitpicking, and it's just supposed to be silly fun, but when there's nothing else to review, what else am I supposed to glom onto. This episode was boring and senseless and I felt it ended before it even got started. Also the worms were never a clear threat, so was Todd essentially the villain? Because of that and many other things the episode felt incomplete, like when you cut off a worm's head, but the rest of it still moves around.

Series Mythology

-Director Steve DiMarco's first of two episodes for the series. He will return for this season's "Ghost Beach".

-Cinematographer Barry Bergthorsen holds the record with forty-two episodes photographed for *Goosebumps*, and he begins that run of episodes with this one.

EP.26:
"You Can't Scare Me"

Airdate: October 5, 1996
Written by: Peter Mitchell
Directed by: René Bonniére
Based on the Goosebumps book: You Can't Scare Me! (#15)

Guest Cast

Charlotte Sullivan   Dylan Provencher
Kiel Campbell   Garry Robbins

Favorite Line:
"She talks like a book."
-Hat

Synopsis

Courtney is the class know-it-all and the class bullies Hat and Eddie plan to take her down a peg or two by giving her a good scare, but they'll find out that getting her to squeal in fear will take a lot more than they bargained for.

Review

This is, in my opinion, the best episode the series has served up so far. It's got a recognizable plotline in keeping with the series formula, but it feels fresh and unique, and it manages to throw in a twist that enhances instead of detracts, making the characters shine instead of the material, which is a good thing.

This is the reverse of "The Haunted Mask". There two bullies were very able to scare the lead gal, but here Courtney is a fearless, know-it-all, teacher's pet with a thick skin. The big difference is that the focus in the episode is not on our heroine, but on the bullies Eddie and Hat; I assume Hat is named Hat because he is the only kid in school who wears one. Essentially, they're not really bullies, they just don't like the attention-seeking antics and the seemingly perfect attitude that Courtney displays. We've all known a

Courtney in our lives, so there is a certain perverse sense of understanding which connects us instantly to Eddie and Hat. The whole point of a *Goosebumps* story is to see yourself as one of the young protagonists and pretend you are experiencing the situation, and this one (while I never put a snake in a girl's lunch) hits close to home for myself.

Here the plot's thrust isn't based on the monster, the threat, but the escalation of scares, or lack thereof. The finale uses its amazing swamp location to its maximum limit, providing a gorgeous background to the Scooby-Doo shenanigans. The twist, which isn't really a big swerve (it's not like we find out Courtney is a Mud Monster), is that Courtney uses her unflappable attitude to talk the Mud Monster to death, drying him up in the sun. This leads to more fame for her, and even more ridicule for Eddie and Hat, and it's simply perfect because it plays effortlessly. I will say the Mud Monster looks a bit

rubbery, especially when it screams and its mouth doesn't move, but beyond that small technical hitch, this episode doesn't muddy the water.

<u>Series Mythology</u>

-Director René Bonniére ends his two-episode run with this one, having previously directed this season's "Be Careful What You Wish for".

-Writer Peter Mitchell turns in his first and only script for *Goosebumps* here.

-Actor Kiel Campbell (Eddie) will return in season three's "The Haunted House Game."

-Actor Dylan Provencher (Hat) will return in season three's "The House of No Return".

-Actor Lucy Peacock returns to the series here after playing the absent mom in season one's two-parter "Stay Out of the Basement".

-The harmless corn snake returns from its brief appearance in season one's "The Werewolf of Fever Swamp", another swamp-set episode.

EP.27:
"Revenge of the Lawn Gnomes"
Airdate: October 12, 1996
Written by: Charles Lazer
Directed by: William Fruet
Based on the Goosebumps book: Revenge of the Lawn Gnomes (#34)

Guest Cast

Lance Paton	Kerry Segal
Peter Keleghan	David Hemblen

Favorite Line:
"Dracula's elves maybe."
-Joe

Synopsis

Joe and Mindy's dad loves to decorate their garden, but when he brings home some giant lawn gnomes to live in their yard, the garden becomes a warzone.

Review

Gnomes are objectively creepy. Even if we look past all the centuries of folk tales and whatnot, the looks on those little ceramic (or plastic) faces is enough to fuel nightmares for ages. My ten-year-old daughter Abby is petrified of gnomes, and we don't even have any in our yard! There is just something inherently unsound about the look and presence of a gnome and here it is capitalized on to great effect.

The gnomes featured in this episode state that their one true purpose is to cause mischief, and so they do by destroying the neighbor's pristine yard and getting our hero, Joe, in trouble. No one will believe him that the gnomes did it, which is crazy because everyone should instantly believe a gnome is capable of anything, and so he takes it upon himself to prove his innocence, and we get a classic heroes journey from inside the world of *Goosebumps*. No time is wasted in showing us the gnomes causing havoc, and believe me when I say I haven't slept well since. They also breed like crazy, because I counted four gnomes toward the end instead of the original two, and there may have been more! Then we come to the twist at the end, which is a satisfying come-uppance as the jerky neighbor, Major McCall, not only discovers the gnomes are alive, but is turned into one of them. Does this mean he'll come to life every night and cause mischief?

Another question this episode left me with is why the gnomes remained in Joe and Mindy's yard at the end. They knew the things were alive and not to be trusted, so why the heck are those things still hanging around? They should have been smashed come morning! Maybe the final moments take place the morning after the big chase, and Joe and Mindy plan to get rid of them later, but if I were them I wouldn't wait on it.   One of the best scenes in the 2015 *Goosebumps* movie involved the lawn gnomes, but they went with the traditional, smaller gnomes; I prefer these giant suckers, they run faster!

Series Mythology

-Little people played the gnomes; Actor Jordan Prentice, who will return later this season as the body of Rocky the dummy in "Night of the Living Dummy 3", and Actor Yvan Labelle played Hap and Chip, respectively, the main gnomes.

-Actor David Hemblen (Major McCall) doesn't return to the series, but he will go on to play other heavies in some very memorable genre fair.

EP.28:
"Ghost Beach"

Airdate: October 19, 1996
Written by: Jeffrey Cohen
Directed by: Steve DiMarco
Based on the Goosebumps book: Ghost Beach (#22)

Guest Cast

Sheldon Smith	Jessica Hogeveen
Bill Turnbull	Anna Majewski

Favorite Line:
"It killed and ate it because dogs can tell if someone's a ghost!"
-Luisa

Synopsis

Siblings Jerry and Terri don't believe that ghosts lurk on the shores of a nearby beach, but they will discover that not everyone they meet is alive... in fact, no one is.

Review

This is the Swiss-cheesiest episode yet. So much nonsense and red-herrings that turn into real plot points that it collapses under its own formulaic weight and zeroes itself out shock-wise. What I mean by this is not only is there one twist, but three, and every guess we've had on who the ghost is is the right guess, so the flow of logic and pacing go out the window and it all becomes ridiculous. They also manage to throw in one last twist where we find out that the old folks Terri and Jerry were staying with are dog-eating ghosts or something like that. What the heck is going? In fact, this episode left me with more questions than a *Star Wars* movie.

Why would ghosts be wearing modern clothing? They didn't have hoodies in colonial times. When Sam and Luisa first meet Jerry and Terri, why would Luisa need to wear a costume to scare them, and where did she get it? Apparently, everyone has a tombstone, so why do they pretend they aren't ghosts? For fun? How did Sam and Luisa make up those Jerry and Terri tombstones, with ghost magic or did they go to Ghost Home Depot? Why does Harrison Sadler say he isn't a ghost, when he clearly is? They've seen his grave and they call him out on it, but then he denies it? Why is Harrison Sadler trapped in the cave? He's a ghost so he can go anywhere! Why do Sam and Luisa want to keep him trapped in the cave with a rock landslide? How are Brad and Agatha ghosts? They cook dinner, have a house, and presumably pay the bills on it, right? Where did that dog come from at the end? It looked like Harrison called him, but didn't it get trapped in the cave with them when the rocks fell? Is it a ghost dog? If so, doesn't that negate the dogs-know-a-ghost if it itself is a ghost? Also, why are Sam and Luisa scared of the dog, don't they eat dogs?

I could go on and on, and but I think the answer to all these giant, bizarre plot holes is the fact that they wanted to trick the audience, even at the expense of logic, and that's a real shame. The story of Sam and Luisa is incredibly sad and tragic, having died young, and that could have been milked to greater effect. Also, the dog-eating old folks are fantastic in their last scene, so that plot point could have been expanded. They chose to deliver a mélange of bluffs and counter bluffs that were actually not dead ends and ultimately it becomes a confused, illogical mess. I watched this episode with my kids, ages ten and three, and even they spotted the inconsistencies. Kids are smart; you shouldn't try to trick kids, so it's better for the story if you don't even try.

Series Mythology

-Director Steve DiMarco ends his two-episode run here, after helming "Go Eat Worms" a few episodes back.

-Writer Jeffrey Cohen ends his run on the series here after penning the two-parter "Welcome to Camp Nightmare" last season.

-Actor Dorothy Gordon (Agatha) doesn't return to *Goosebumps*, but her first TV appearance was as the original voice of Piglet and Christopher Robin in the 1952 *Winnie-the-Pooh* series.

EP.29:
"Attack of the Jack-O'-Lanterns"

<u>Airdate</u>: October 26, 1996
<u>Written by</u>: Dan Angel & Billy Brown
<u>Directed by</u>: William Fruet
<u>Based on the Goosebumps book</u>: <u>Attack of the Jack-O'-Lanterns</u> (#48)

<u>Guest Cast</u>

Erica Luttrell	Aidan Desalaiz
Maria Paikin	Gino Giacomini

<u>Favorite Line:</u>
"A better place!"
-The Pumpkinheads

Synopsis

A pair of Pumpkin-headed monsters take a group of kids to the ultimate neighborhood where they clean up on candy, but when they try to leave they discover that the monsters want them to trick or treat forever!

Review

I love a good Halloween episode, and here they've spared no expense on the decoration budget. I just wish the plot was a little better, and didn't rely on constantly pulling the rug out from under us.

Drew and Walker want to get back at Tabitha and Lee, the jerks who constantly play pranks on them, and Drew's old friends Shane and Shana, who are visiting from out of town, offer to help them. Already there are a ton of kids to keep track of, and the story hasn't kicked off properly yet! Then we experience this really bizarre, extended nightmare sequence where a freaky old couple kidnaps the gang, but it never pays off or connects to anything, and wasted too much screen time for no reason, so we'll just move on to the meat of the episode.

The plan is for Drew and Walker to take Tabitha and Lee trick or treating and leave the pranking to Shane and Shana, but during said adventure they get kidnapped by pumpkin-headed monsters and taken to a magical Halloween neighborhood where they are forced to trick or treat forever, which I guess is a form of punishment. The big babies get tired and Tabitha and Lee run away like little scaredy-cats. The pumpkin creatures reveal themselves to be Shane and Shana all along. And how did they do all this? Simple, it's *Goosebumps* so they are obviously aliens!

The aliens say that Halloween is the one time a year they get to be someone else, but then they remove their human heads and you see that they're really green, worm things, so aren't they pretending to be humans the whole time, negating the specialness of Halloween? Not to mention the NEXT twist where the aliens reveal they eat humans and wouldn't be against eating their pal, Drew! So to recap: the pumpkin creatures were real, but they were really Shane and Shana in disguise, and Shane and Shana are really aliens, but they're really not humans, but worm aliens who eat humans. My head is spinning! This is just another example of extra layers of twist that ruin a story, like that extra ingredient that destroys the soup; it's just a bit too much.

I love the setting and the art direction, plus the pumpkin creatures looked pretty great, but the overall package was, to use an applicable metaphor, like eating a whole bag of Halloween candy, which is not a great idea.

<u>Series Mythology</u>

-Actor Erica Luttrell (Drew) returns to the series after her brief appearance in season one's "Piano Lessons Can Be Murder".

-Actor Andrea O'Roarke (Shana) loves Halloween because she will return in an uncredited role in the next episode, "The Haunted Mask 2".

-Actor Philip Eddolls (Shane) returns to the series after his work on the stage in season one's "The Phantom of the Auditorium".

EP.30:
"The Haunted Mask 2 Pt.1"
Airdate: October 29, 1996
Written by: William Fruet
Directed by: Dan Angel & Billy Brown
Based on the Goosebumps book: The Haunted Mask 2 (#36)

Guest Cast

John White	Amos Crawley
Kathryn Long	Kathryn Short

Favorite Line:
"Why don't you go home? I don't want to see your crybaby face."
-Steve (as the Haunted Mask)

Synopsis
The season of the witch resurrects the buried Haunted Mask, who leads an unsuspecting boy to the mask shop where a new mask, in the form of a rotting old man, finds a home on his face.

Review
R.L. Stine returns to introduce the first of a handful of sequels the series tackled. This episode follows the Halloween-themed "Attack of the Jack-O'-Lanterns", and it even opens almost exactly like that previous episode, speaking toward the formulaic nature of the series, but this time the tables are turned because Carly Beth is no longer the scaredy-cat we met in part one. This being a sequel to the first episode in the series, there is a lot riding on it. Luckily, it manages to deliver the same feels, but give us a new twist on the haunted mask concept.

This sequel feels more balanced and paced than the first one, seeing as we don't have to use up screen time on showcasing Carly Beth's fears. This one cuts to the quick right out of the gate and develops naturally. There's some heavy foreshadowing where Steve laments that life is passing him by and that before he knows it he'll be a "drooling, disgusting old man", which is exactly what he becomes on this most auspices Halloween for him. That moment and Steve's need to scare people are about it for character development, but that's really all we need.

Carly Beth and Sabrina appear in the episode, but are sidelined because they aren't the leads anymore. However, I appreciated that they kept the same actors for the roles, which had become iconic to an extent. They'll have more to do in the second-half, but for this first part, it's strictly Steve's shows. He has the same goals as Carly Beth had in the original, but he follows a new trajectory when it comes to the unsavory haunted aspects of the mask.

The reworking of the original mask as the mastermind who helps the other masks find faces is really unique, and in keeping with the first one. This new mask, the old man, is markedly different. He's up for chaos, but he's also got major emphysema and whatnot like a real old man would, and so his story arc is different and unique from the original mask's journey. That one was all about causing havoc, but this one exists to serve the original mask, and we'll get into more of that later. This was a really strong, confident first half with no wasted elements that might even work better than the original's first half, however it benefits from the setup in the original so it balances out.

<u>Series Mythology</u>

-Actor John White steps into the role of Steve after original actor George Kinamis exited, and takes the lead in this episode after battling time itself in season one's "The Cuckoo Clock of Doom".

-Actors Kathryn Long (Carly Beth), Kathryn Short (Sabrina), Colin Fox (Shopkeeper), Amos Crawley (Chuck), and Brenda Bazinet (Carly's Mom Kate) return to reprise their roles from the original, and bid a fond adieu to the series as well.

-Actor Scott Wickware plays the man in the haunted mask, doubling for the Shopkeeper. We last saw him as the Masked Mutant in this season's "Attack of the Mutant" and we shall see him again later this season in "Welcome to Dead House".

-Actor Andrea O'Roarke plays an uncredited role here after playing an alien in the last episode, "Attack of the Jack-O'-Lanterns". I believe she played the painter girl, who has her candy stolen by Steve the old man.

EP.31:
"The Haunted Mask 2 Pt.2"

<u>Airdate</u>: October 29, 1996
<u>Written by</u>: William Fruet
<u>Directed by</u>: Dan Angel & Billy Brown
<u>Based on the Goosebumps book</u>: The Haunted Mask 2 (#36)

Guest Cast

John White	Amos Crawley
Kathryn Long	Kathryn Short

Favorite Line:
"Oh, you smell, Mister."
-Football Player Kid

Synopsis
Steve discovers the haunted mask's side effects and is enslaved by the original haunted mask until his friends can come to his rescue.

Review
The second half sees the fallout from wearing the haunted mask, and Steve is less than prepared for it. What starts out as just an ungodly thirst, turns into a gasping near-death and mutated old-man-hands that put him under the control of the original mask (I wish these guys had names so it wouldn't be so confusing). He commands Steve to steal Carly Beth's ceramic head from her house; it's her symbol of love and he needs to destroy it. Steve sneaks into Carly Beth's house, manages to grab it, and smashes it to pieces in the cemetery for the original mask.

Meanwhile, Carly Beth, Sabrina, and Chuck are searching for Steve. No one believes her, but Carly Beth knows that Steve is in serious trouble. They meet up with Steve and the original mask in the cemetery, and thanks to the smashed ceramic head, Carly Beth is now in mortal danger of being repossessed by the original mask. The day is saved when Steve pushes Carly Beth out of the way and head butts the original mask, somehow defeating it at the stroke of midnight by what was apparently a self-sacrificing symbol of love. This isn't the most believable climax, and it felt a bit too rushed and neat, but I can see the need for efficiency when it comes to keeping all of this within the length of the episode. The dour, downbeat ending where everyone looked defeated, instead of cheerful, felt right and earned, and added to the realism of the characters for me, as well.

The direction from William Fruet and the writing from Dan Angel and Billy Brown are on point and make this the most satisfying two-parter. The stakes are high, the plot is nearly flawless, and the way it connects to the original is rewarding. There also isn't a goofy twist to undo the works, so I'm grateful for what is a straightforward tale that fires on all cylinders. All in all, I would say "The Haunted Mask 2" was better than the first one, with an expansion of the world and the mythology of the mask, and a solid use of all the characters in play. The episode ends with us discovering that R.L. Stine loves the cream-filled Halloween candies the best, so isn't that a nice treat?

Series Mythology

-Actor Bucky Hill (Football Player kid) will return to the series in season three's two-parter "Werewolf Skin".

-Actor Hamille Rustia plays an uncredited character here, but will return twice more in the series in bigger roles. We will see her next this season in "Calling All Creeps!" and later as the lead in the season four two-parter "Cry of the Cat".

-Actor Trevor Wilson plays an uncredited teen here, and will return for another uncredited appearance in season three's "My Best Friend Is Invisible".

-Actor Cody Jones (Carly Beth's brother Noah) will return to the series in season four's "The Ghost Next Door".

EP. 32:

"Let's Get Invisible"

Airdate: November 2, 1996

Written by: Rick Drew

Directed by: Ron Oliver

Based on the Goosebumps book: Let's Get Invisible (#6)

Guest Cast

Kevin Zegers   Flora Chu

Jonathan Schwartz   Adam Bonneau

Favorite Line:

"Left-handers rule."

-Noah

Synopsis

Max and his pals discover a secret room hiding a mysterious mirror that causes invisibility, but its true purpose is more nefarious than first imagined.

Review

On first appraisal, this is all pretty goofy. I use that word a lot when it comes to *Goosebumps*, but while this word describes my initial impression, the implications of the plot are vast and mortifying. If you're going in believing you are about to see an episode concerning invisible antics, you'll be sadly mistaken, but that's the good news. This episode isn't just a take on invisibility; in fact, it isn't a take on invisibility at all! This episode is concerned with the weaponization of your own reflection, with the invisibility aspect being really just the sugar that attracts the flies.

There's a lot to unpack here concerning the mirror universe and the evil doppelgangers and the invisibility side effects, but we don't really get any concrete answers, and that makes complete sense within the framework of the story, so I won't bother analyzing how the mirror got into Max's house, or how it works. We can presuppose the mirror is a trap to lure folks into this alternate world, where an evil version of yourself exists and wants to trade places with you. This evil version is most likely a reflection of all the hate, anger, and bad juju inside us, and in a way the mirror takes away your plain reflection with the invisibility in the hopes of replacing it with a version of you that is pure id. This was certainly a deeper concept than I was expecting and I was very impressed with the proceedings.

This is a swiftly paced episode deftly handled by writer Rick Drew and director Ron Oliver. It is a pretty low-budget episode, since it almost entirely takes place in the attic with the mirror, but that's where the action is. The mirror world also looked a little shoddy, but maybe this was a rushed production with no money or time to really shoot the works on the freezing mirror world. The cast is ok, with no real standouts, but decent work throughout. Overall, this was a very unique episode. Not a series highlight, but one that delivered a story that used some creative out-of-the-box thinking, and I'm grateful for that.

The episode ends with a cliffhanger/twist with Noah being his mirror version, and while we don't know what the mirror personas want, we assume Max's life isn't going to get any less strange. This twist is paid off because they kept mentioning that Noah was a lefty, which I found really odd at first. Another thing I found odd production-wise, and maybe it was just my impression, but why were Max and Noah's parents so old-looking?

<u>Series Mythology</u>

-Director Ron Oliver cameos as one of the mirror world's victims; he's the one screaming while pulling down a yellow hat on his head.

-Actors Flora Chu (Erin), Adam Bonneau (Zack), and Eve Crawford (Mrs. Thompson) never return to *Goosebumps*, but they are also all alumni of *Are You Afraid of the Dark?*

-Max is basically wearing a *Goosebumps* cap throughout the third-act of the episode. It's supposed to symbolize the G for his baseball team the Giants, but we all know that font very well by now, don't we?

EP.33:

"Scarecrow Walks at Midnight"

Airdate: November 9, 1996

Written by: Scott Peters

Directed by: Randy Bradshaw

Based on the Goosebumps book: The Scarecrow Walks at Midnight (#20)

Guest Cast

Heather Bertram	John E. Campbell
Bob Clout	Louise Nicol

Favorite Line:

"You city kids sure scare easy."

-Sticks

Synopsis

While visiting their grandparents' farm, Jodie and Mark discover that not only are things very different than they used to be, but the scarecrows walk at midnight.

Review

At first I thought this was going to be a take on the famous *Twilight Zone* episode "It's a Good Life", where a small boy holds a town hostage due to a combination of magic powers and emotional volatility, when we meet Stanley the farm hand and everyone seemed to be deferring to him; even grandma and grandpa, his supposed bosses, seem scared of him. Turns out it isn't as interesting as all that; it's a bit sillier than a boy with magic powers and a bad attitude.

The scarecrows are alive! They're alive because the simple-minded Stanley found a book of magic spells and used it to give life to the scarecrows to help him in the fields. Now, they won't stay asleep, and for some reason they want to terrorize those nearby. Maybe it's just me, but I don't consider Scarecrows inherently evil, so why would they have a thirst for menace? As far as scarecrows-come-to-life stories, I have to be honest and say this is pretty subpar. What with it's vague excuse for the living scarecrows and its lack of motivation plot and logic-wise, this is basically just an excuse to have scarecrows running around, and that's kind of disappointing.

The cast is exceptionally good here, however, with Michael Copeman's Stanley as the standout. The lead kids Heather Bertram (Jodie) and John E. Campbell (Mark) are really pretty good in this and make the proceedings a little easier to swallow. I guess my main complaint, despite the fact that a random magic spell made them come to life, is that I don't understand why the scarecrows want to attack the family. It's small thing, but a crucial thing. Sure, the finale is fun, fast-paced, and full of monster goodness, but if it's all for vague reasons then it's like looking for a needle in a haystack, pointless.

<u>Series Mythology</u>

-Actor Michael Copeman (Stanley) does not return to the series, but he did appear in an episode of *Are You Afraid of the Dark?* titled "The Tale of the Fire Ghost".

-Actor Kris "Chris" Lemche (Sticks) does not return to the series either, but did appear in an episode of *Eerie, Indiana: The Other Dimension* titled "The Goody Two-Shoes People".

-For some reason, the episode's title is subtly different than the book's, which reads <u>The Scarecrow Walks at Midnight.</u>

EP.34:

"Monster Blood"

Airdate: November 16, 1996
Written by: Rick Drew
Directed by: Timothy Bond
Based on the Goosebumps book: Monster Blood (#3)

Guest Cast

Kyle Labine	Sarah Podemski
Corinne Conley	Joy Tanner

Favorite Line:

"Andy, Evan's friend? Are your related to the Chicago Evansfriends?"
-Aunt Katherine

Synopsis

Evan discovers a jar of green slime in a room in his Great Aunt's house, and he quickly discovers why she had forbidden him to enter that room.

Review

This is one of the most fun episodes in the season, and the perfect one for the Nickelodeon generation thanks to all that green slime. Said green slime is the monster blood and, while we never find out which monster bled out to provide it, it acts like a catalyst for all the weird stuff that's about to happen. Never mind the answers to our questions, the monster blood can do anything from make animals grow to devour humans in one bite... or gulp... or maybe slurp?

This episode starts with the common trope of a new kid in a new house, but instead of ghosts or whatnot, his aunt forbids him to enter this specific room, which is a blatant invitation to do so. He meets a girl from the neighborhood and to prove to her that he isn't scared they sneak into the room and discover a jar of slime labeled "Monster Blood". Of course the first thing they do is play with the stuff, what with a name like that. At the moment the jar was opened, a ghost cat was let free, and we'll get to her in a minute. The slime then begins to grow and overwhelms the house, and soon Aunt Katherine discovers the untenable situation.

Here we get the goofiest elements, and you knew they were coming folks, when the cat morphs into a witch and threatens to sick her monster blood on them. Aunt Katherine explains that the witch was a boarder who she caught practicing black magic in her room and when she tried to kick her out, the witch got swallowed up by the slime, and Aunt Katherine then decided to lock her up forever in that unused room. This doesn't make much sense until you see what the monster blood can do in the sequel, which was originally created for the series only. Anyway, the day is saved when Evan's dog, who swallowed the slime, arrives as a towering giant and scares the cat witch into the slime thusly canceling both of them out somehow. This ending felt a bit rushed and too easy, but I loved the giant dog effects, so it didn't really hinder my enjoyment.

There is a great moment I love when Evan and Andy first meet and they share an awkward handshake; it's a nice, subtle bit of business that felt organic and real. I like to see those moments on screen because it makes the characters come alive, and not feel scripted or rehearsed. This whole episode felt fresh and unique, and partly that was due to the casting. The young kids are great, but the standout is Corinne Conley (Aunt Katherine), who hams it up, but does a nice job regardless, and reminds me of the weirdo witch from *Troll 2* (if you've seen that movie, you know who I mean, and if you haven't seen that movie, then finish this whole book first, AND THEN go see *Troll 2*). The episode ends with a cliffhanger that was never supposed to be paid off, but we will see the monster blood in action again as the team reunites to give us "More Monster Blood" next episode, but if this were a standalone it would still be a pretty fun one.

Series Mythology

-While we will never see Aunt Katherine and Andy again, actors Kyle Labine (Evan), Ashley Dawn Brown (Julia), and Mark Benesh (Curtis) will return for the plane-centric sequel next episode.

EP.35:

"More Monster Blood"

Airdate: November 16, 1996

Written by: Dan Angel & Billy Brown, Rick Drew

Directed by: Timothy Bond

Guest Cast

Kyle Labine
Charles Boyland
Ashley Dawn Brown
Mark Benesh

Favorite Line:

"Airline food makes the monster blood sick!"

-Curtis

Synopsis

Evan returns home to his parents, but unbeknownst to him a bit of monster blood has stowed away on the plane with him.

Review

Was this episode an inventive use of a rented set, or a brilliant masterstroke in world building? Either way, it's a really fun, claustrophobic monster mash, and it not only works as a continuation of the first "Monster Blood", but as a solid standalone sequel as well, which cannot be said for most two-parters. Based on an original concept, this time the slime goes wild forty thousand miles up in the air, eating passengers and causing mayhem. Seeing how easy it was for the slime to devour a human, we can now see how the monster blood could have consumed the witch Sarabeth from last episode. However, Evan and Andy had been playing with the stuff like it was Flubber, so why didn't it eat them? This series isn't without it's holes, so I won't bother to patch it up here, because it's enjoyable enough, and no one can provide a valid scientific explanation on monster blood traits anyway.

This tight, contained episode uses its limited area to up the suspense and tension, and gives our young cast some real challenges to tackle. Some time is spent with the three new kids, summer campers returning home, and I credit writer Rick Drew (working from a story by Dan Angel & Billy Brown) for giving us some well-drawn characters. This time around, the slime grows fast and furious and they'll have to use their ingenuity to stop it before it takes the plane down. The writers use their set to their advantage and incorporate the overhead bins to make their final strike on the slimeball, and while the overhead bins are not ever open tunnels as depicted, because the luggage would fly around all over during takeoff and landing, I'll let the small leap in reality pass. The use of airline food as the monster blood's weakness is yet another brilliant bit of situational problem solving, and incorporates the location organically, even if it does still feel pretty rushed.

This episode is a perfect sequel, and shouldn't be considered a second-half to "Monster Blood". Only Evan returns and the location is very different, so to me that feels more like a sequel. Not to mention the fact that R.L. Stine didn't write anything like this, so it most assuredly can be considered a spin-off standalone, but it also enriches the first "Monster Blood" at the same time. We still don't know much about the monster blood's origins, or the extent of its powers, which so far have included swamping humans and making animals grow to gargantuan size, and since we will never see the monster

blood in live-action again, you'll have to turn to the book series to see where Evan and the monster blood meet again.

<u>Series Mythology</u>

-While there are four <u>Monster Blood</u> novels by R.L. Stine as of this writing, this episode is an original spin-off from the first part. The real sequels were never made into an episode, but elements are shared between them, including the recurring character of Conan, the bully.

-The original title to this episode was "Flight Monster Blood", which would have been amazing, and sounds even more like a sequel/spin-off title.

-This episode is the first of four original episodes created strictly for the TV series. We won't see the other three until next season with the "Chillogy" trilogy.

EP.36:

"Vampire Breath"

Airdate: November 23, 1996

Written by: Rick Drew

Directed by: Ron Oliver

Based on the Goosebumps book: Vampire Breath (#49)

Guest Cast

Zach "Zack" Lipovsky   Meredith Henderson

Earl Pastko   Krista Dufresne

Favorite Line:

"I get the top coffin."

-Freddy

Synopsis

While searching their home for their birthday presents, twins Freddy and Cara discover a secret door that leads to the underground lair of Count Nightwing, king of the vampires.

Review

I'm not sure what R.L. Stine's obsession is with kids stuck in a house, but the typical, formulaic *Goosebumps* episode is given a blood transfusion here for the better, pun intended. Freddy and Cara's birthday present treasure hunt turns into *The Goonies* meets *The Monster Squad* as they uncover a hidden room that leads to a cavern deep below their town that is stacked high with the bloodthirsty dead. You would think the vampire problem would be a big deal in their town, but they seemed as surprised as I was to witness the breadth of the undead's reign.

The young cast is fine, and Earl Pastko as Count Nightwing gives a restrained and controlled performance, but it's the sets that really stick in my memory. That cave set that looked lit like an amusement park haunted house ride was amazing, layered, and very detailed; kudos to the art team. The concept of vampire breath as a way for the vampires to store their essence to help them regenerate is interesting, but since it really isn't explored in details, it comes off more like a MacGuffin than anything else.

I wish the pacing and the scope had been tweaked, because the story seemed too compact and slight to even fit a whole *Goosebumps* book, and I'm sure stuff was cut out, but I wish the locations had been expanded a bit. As it stands the episode is a fun watch, but it feels like its over before it's begun, and the minimal use of spaces is really the issue at hand there. Also, this one is hindered and helped by the *Goosebumps* tropes. It is hindered because the moment we meet Gwendolyn, and she says she isn't a vampire, we know instantly she's lying and can't be trusted; further, since the parents are gone for most of the episode and return right at the end, you know something weird is up with them so the reveal that they are vampires as well loses its shock value. The episode is however helped by the tropes, because the final twist with the family bloodline actually enriches the plot and doesn't knock the story past the bleachers. It makes sense within the context of the story and the world, so we can be grateful for that much, and forgive its sameness.

Series Mythology

-Freddy and Cara's last name is a reference to Dracula's obsessed sidekick, Renfield, from the original novel by Bram Stoker.

-Actor Meredith Henderson (Cara) will not return to the series, but she will act with another *Goosebumps* alum when she appears in the film *Jumper* with Hayden Christensen, who will appear later this season in "Night of the Living Dummy 3", and is also better known as young Darth Vader.

EP.37:

"How to Kill a Monster"

<u>Airdate</u>: May 1, 1997

<u>Written by</u>: Ron Oliver

<u>Directed by</u>: Ron Oliver

Based on the Goosebumps book: <u>How to Kill a Monster</u> (#46)

Guest Cast

Courtney Hawkrigg　　　　　　　　Ricky Mabe

Helen Hughes　　　　　　　　　　Peter Boretski

Favorite Line:

"It's dark up there. It might be dangerous. You go first."

-Clark

Synopsis

Brand new stepsiblings head to the swamps to spend the weekend with their grandparents, only to find themselves in a fight for their lives against a mutant swamp creature that they just so happen to be locked in the house with.

Review

How DO you kill a monster? Ever wonder? Well, watch this episode and find out! Again, we have the old standby of fish-out-of-water kids being introduced to a new house of horrors; these setups are getting repetitive now.

I feel like most of the episodes have become self-contained in one or two locations for some reason. Maybe the budgets were dropping in season two? Gretchen and Clark, newly brother and sister thanks to their parents getting hitched, are stranded at Gretchen's grandparents house while their folks are on their honeymoon. One day they find themselves locked into the house with a creature that looks like one of Godzilla's foes, and they'll either have to kill it, or let it kill them. They try everything from causing it to fall from a great height, and cooking up a batch of ridiculously spicy Gumbo for it, but ultimately t'was man's germs (ala <u>War of the Worlds</u>) that killed the beast, because Clark's last ditch effort is to shove his arm down the monster's throat for some unknown reason, and his germ-ridden arm destroys it.

Here I have to hand it to the creative team because the episode avoids a few clichéd moments that I thought it was heading toward. The premise is very straightforward, with no big swerve-twists to get in the way. Clark and Gretchen are locked into a house with a monster and they have to kill it; easy, done. I thought for sure the grandparents would be monsters, but they play a very minimal part in all of this, which is a shame because I loved Peter Boretski as Grandpa Eddie, and would have loved to see more.

This is basically *Home Alone* with a monster. It's another swamp-set episode, so I'm wondering if they had easy access to swamp stuff, or if it was tricky to find in Canada. The chemistry between Courtney Hawkrigg (Gretchen) and Ricky Mabe (Clark) is pretty solid and you buy that they've come closer together as brother and sister by the end. Also, we get an answer to one of our burning *Goosebumps* questions: when the monster in this is finally defeated, it explodes and sprays them with a greenish, slimy blood… MONSTER BLOOD! We've found our culprit.

Series Mythology

-Director Ron Oliver's first of a handful of episodes where he handles the writing duties as well. His next written and directed episode will be season four's two-parter "How I Got My Shrunken Head".

-Actor Ricky Mabe (Clark) will not return to *Goosebumps*, but does appear later in an episode of *Are You Afraid of the Dark?*

EP. 38:
"Calling All Creeps"

Airdate: June 15, 1997
Written by: Dan Angel & Billy Brown
Directed by: Craig Pryce
Based on the Goosebumps book: Calling All Creeps! (#50)

Guest Cast

Zachary Carlin	Hamille Rustia
Maia Filar	Matthew Lemche

Favorite Line:
"Humans are the past. Creeps are the future."
-David, Brenda & Wart

Synopsis
After a prank backfires at school, Ricky uncovers a hidden group of monsters posing as fellow students with plans on world domination.

Review
Ricky is a downtrodden, clichéd nerdy kid and he's had it. He's tired of being pushed around and made fun of, so he begins a counterstrike against the jerks at school by targeting his main tormentor Tasha, the head of the school newspaper, first. He writes up an ad to appear in the paper calling for all the creeps who see it to give Tasha a call after midnight. What kind of creeps does he mean? I supposed he imagined weirdoes and kooks, but when Tasha catches wind of the ad and changes it to his name and number, he starts to get calls from something else.

It turns out his school has been infiltrated by yellow dragon monsters, or aliens, or lizard people, or something. Regardless of their genus, they are sure creepy, and they believe Ricky has come forward as their leader to finally plan the takeover of mankind. The three creeps just so happened to be three of the biggest bullies at school, ones who used to pick on him, but are now under his command, and if he doesn't follow through on their plans to mutate the entire school into creeps, then he'll become their lunch. This episode explores the old adage "Absolute power corrupts absolutely", when Ricky is faced with saving his taunting classmates or sitting back and watching them turn into creeps that will surely treat him like a king. It's a great, moral dilemma set in a *Goosebumps* world, and the ending is both tragic and satisfying. You do kind of feel bad for Iris, Ricky's only friend, who remains human and is shocked by Ricky's change; she's most likely going to be on the menu soon.

Speaking of that ending, there are a few things that don't make sense. Firstly, as soon as this kids change (as seen from the reflection in Ricky's glasses) they all start chanting his name, but why the heck would they? No power structure has been established, so no one knows that Ricky is the commander. They should all be too busy freaking out that they're creeps now. Secondly, Wart hands Ricky a cookie to help him transform, but why the heck would he do that? Don't they believe Ricky is already a creep? If they knew he was just a human, they wouldn't have followed his so-called plans. So if they believed he was a creep, why would he need a cookie? Lastly, if the creeps were just waiting for their commander to arrive, and Ricky unwittingly took his place, then where is the real commander? This episode left too many things unanswered, and it speaks to the open-ended nature of the material, but I wish there was a follow-up to see what the fallout would have been. Oh well, we can dream one up ourselves!

Series Mythology

-Director Craig Pryce's first and only time helming an episode.

-Actors Hamille Rustia (Iris), Diana Salvatore (Tasha's Friend), and Colleen Williams (Mrs. Urick) will all return for season four's two-parter "Cry of the Cat".

-Actor Matthew Lemche (David) will return in the season three episode "Click", and is the brother of Kris Lemche, who battled walking straw in "Scarecrow Walks at Midnight".

EP.39:
"Welcome to Dead House Pt.1"

Airdate: June 29, 1997
Written by: Dan Angel & Billy Brown
Directed by: William Fruet
Based on the Goosebumps book: Welcome to Dead House (#1)

Guest Cast

Amy Stewart	Ben Cook
Elizabeth Saunders	Benedict Campbell

Favorite Line:
"Hey, money!"

-Josh

Synopsis

A family moves into a new home in a new town, and they discover that the town's infrastructure isn't the only thing that's dead around here.

Review

Finally, the first ever Goosebumps novel has been adapted, and while they thought they needed two parts to tell this tale, I think condensing it into one would have been the better play, because this first section is all first-act setup and to be honest it's really kind of dull. I understand the need for setting up tension and dread, but when you think about it, nothing really happens here at all. Now, I understand the MacGuffin of the weird wreath that keeps the family safe, but it slows the plot down and all we get is innocuous scare sequence after innocuous scare sequence with no momentum or weight.

Let's take a closer look at Amanda and Josh and their family's decision to move to this town. They must be ridiculously poor, because the house they move into is utterly disgusting; it's almost crackhouse-level. They seem relatively well off, even if the dad is a struggling writer (believe me, I know how that feels financially), but I think they would have taken one look at that dilapidated pile of junk called a house and booked it the other way. No one in his or her right mind would stay in that stained, rotting, and loosely boarded together shack.

There really isn't much to say about this episode, except that it's probably the flimsiest of the first halves. There is zero story or character development, and the weird thing is that this would have been fine in a feature where we would get to care about these guys, but as a TV show we understand this will be an ephemeral experience, so just get on with it and show us the goods! I will say that Ben Cook (Josh) is the best thing about this entire two-parter, and he's got the right attitude for it, too.

<u>Series Mythology</u>

-Actor Ben Cook (Josh) will return to the series in season three for "A Shocker on Shock Street".

-Makeup FX artist Matthew Galliford cameos here as a ghost in a window.

EP.40:
"Welcome to Dead House Pt.2"

<u>Airdate</u>: June 29, 1997

<u>Written by</u>: Dan Angel & Billy Brown

<u>Directed by</u>: William Fruet

<u>Based on the Goosebumps book</u>: <u>Welcome to Dead House</u> (#1)

Guest Cast

Amy Stewart	Ben Cook
Elizabeth Saunders	Benedict Campbell

Favorite Line:

"Now I know why everyone around here wore hats!"

-Josh

Synopsis

Josh and Amanda discover the town's undead secret and are tricked into destroying the one thing that is keeping them safe, leaving them to fend off against the bloodthirsty townsfolk.

Review

Finally, this thing gets good, and it goes from zero to sixty, folks. The episode starts with some filler as Josh and Amanda go looking for their missing dog, and stumble upon a town meeting where they overhear the dusty, grey-colored folks talking about feeding on the Benson family. Now THIS should have been the cliffhanger of first half, because now this second part has to work like the second and third act all in one, and for the most part it manages well.

The bizarre wreath the mother hung up in their house is the turning point of the whole episode. A family of zombies make their grey zombie look disappear long enough to trick the Benson family (but most likely the audience) into thinking that they are alive and healthy, and convince them to burn the wreath, which must be attracting the living dead. Good old Dad does as asked, and of course the opposite happens, because for some reason the wreath was keeping them safe from the zombies. Now the zombies storm the house and the family has to flee for shelter, but these zombies are crazy and will burst through the walls like the Kool-Aid Man just to get a bite of them. Ultimately, sunlight kills these zombies, which isn't technically part of the zombie rules, but since we don't get a clear explanation about these zombies, or what caused them, I suppose sunlight was just a Deus Ex-Machina to kill them all at once.

And let's talk about these zombies. These guys have to be the laziest, most old-fashioned zombies since the 40s; they look almost like Haunted Mansion ghosts, and that isn't very scary. It's implied the chemical spill in town caused this, but did it also turn everyone silver? And why can't they leave the town and find fresh meat? Seems like incredibly hard work to just rent out abandoned houses and hope big families will come to stay? What's preventing them from heading to New York and putting their foodie hat on? The end may have been exciting, but it also left too many questions, and ultimately came off as silly and kind of disappointing. It all felt so random and dull, which prevented anything from connecting with me.

I would say that this episode pulled its punches more than any other. The zombies were boring, the plotting was labored, and the chills and thrills were anything but. I like a good zombie anything, really, but this was like a zombie story written and produced by people who had no idea what a zombie was.

Series Mythology

-Actor Scott Wickware (Hard Hat Worker) returns here for the last time, after playing the Masked Mutant and the Haunted Mask this season.

-Actor Daniel McGraw did a ton of uncredited work, but deserves a shout out because of the shows he worked on. He plays an uncredited Little Boy in this two-parter, and later plays uncredited parts in three episodes of *Are You Afraid of the Dark?*

-The staircase set during the finale looks like the staircase that led to the first of many deaths for the monster in this season's "How to Kill a Monster".

EP.41:

"Don't Wake Mummy"

<u>Airdate</u>: July 12, 1997
<u>Written by</u>: Rick Drew
<u>Directed by</u>: William Fruet

<u>Based on the Goosebumps book</u>: "Don't Wake Mummy" (Even More Tales to Give You Goosebumps)

Guest Cast

Evan Morgan	A.J. Cook
Lea-Helen Weir	Fiona Reid

Favorite Line:

"It's not creepy, it's just a mummy."
-Mom

Synopsis

When a mummy is delivered to Jeff's house, his sister Kim uses it to torture him, but unwittingly awakens the four-thousand-year old dead guy, who happens to get out on the wrong side of the sarcophagus.

Review

    Yet another housebound episode finds an unlikely enemy going up against an antagonistic brother and sister. I never would have imagined a mummy, of all things, loose in a lovely home in a quiet suburb, but here we are. I wonder if R.L. Stine had a bet with himself about how many stories he could set in a domestic situation, and I would say he most likely holds the record when it comes to stories told in homes.

    The meat of the episode is that Jeff is a total wiener and his sister Kim understandably uses his incredible fearfulness to her advantage and scares him every chance she gets. When their father, an Egyptologist, sends their mother a sarcophagus to study at her leisure, Kim sees it as a perfect thing to use to scare the dickens out of him again. The problem is that when she opens the sarcophagus, she awakens the mummy, and as we all know mummies always wake up angry and wanting to kill anyone around them instantly, no matter what.

The mummy doesn't really get to do much until the end, so the real monster here is Kim, and her utter dislike for her weak, gentle brother, who is probably easier to startle than a baby, and yes actor Evan Morgan (Jeff) does take all that a bit too far. I will say I really loved A.J. Cook (Kim) in this; she was really fun to watch as the plotting and scheming villainess, and she's gone on to have a great career. The mom was pretty terrible as a mom, however, because she let Kim get away with teasing her brother, and was more interested in them just shutting up, than actually solving their sibling issues.

The episode in general is a by-the-numbers affair, but none of it is dull, so I can give it that much. My favorite part was the black and white mummy movie the kids were watching, which was impressively made. The ending, with the ridiculously fake looking mummy cat, really takes it down a few notches, though. I wish I could say the shoddiness of that prop was charming, but I wouldn't want to lie to you, folks.

Series Mythology

-The mummy costume in this episode is not only the same as the one in season one's "The Return of the Mummy", but the same actor, Peter Jarvis, slips into the bandages yet again; most likely because he fit his old costume, but he's a pretty darn good mummy, too. Does this mean that both mummies are the same mummies, or do all mummies have a glazed right eye in *Goosebumps* land? We may never know.

-This episode was filmed during the production of season three, but was aired during season two for some unknown reason.

-Apparently, the house in this episode is the same as the one in this season's "Vampire Breath".

EP.42:
"The Blob That Ate Everyone"
<u>Airdate</u>: July 19, 1997
<u>Written by</u>: Charles Lazer
<u>Directed by</u>: Randy Bradshaw
<u>Based on the Goosebumps book</u>: The Blob That Ate Everyone (#55)

Guest Cast

Scott Pietrangelo	Gabrielle Boni
Bradie Whetham	Marium Carvell

Favorite Line:
"Fresh meat. Fresh meat."
-Adam

Synopsis
A magic typewriter unleashes young author Zack's wildest imagination, which includes a man-eating blob.

Review

I don't think I've really thought this about other stories, but I feel this one should have gotten a two-parter, because this episode ends before it really had a chance to begin. The whole thing hinges on that dang blob that eats everyone, and it only eats one kid, and is defeated almost immediately, and then five seconds later the credits roll. I thought I must have fallen asleep and missed a whole chunk, so I watched it again and confirmed that it was as disappointing as I thought it was.

Zach finds an old typewriter in some abandoned store, and it just so happens to have magic powers; everything he types comes true. This is a premise that can be traced back to a Stephen King story titled "Word Processor of the Gods", and was even plumed by *Are You Afraid of the Dark?* in 1991 with the episode "The Tale of the Dream Machine". It's not a necessarily original concept, but it's all in what you do with it that matters. The King and

Dark? versions are pretty satisfying, but here the concept is only explored minimally, only to be subverted in the end with the real power coming from young Zack's brain, instead of the typewriter. Zack uses his visible brainwaves to wish the blob away, and that's our ending, however if he ALWAYS had this power, why did he need the typewriter to unleash it? He was writing before, so why didn't this happen then? Taking the power away from the typewriter is completely illogical, and makes for a lazy way to end the episode.

There's a bizarre stagecoach joke that no kid would use, or even really understand. I bring that up as an example of the disconnect here with the material and the audience. Too much time is spent testing the typewriter the night before the blob is let loose, especially when it amounts to nothing except proof. The blob looked great and I wish there had been more time spent with it causing chaos and, oh I don't know, maybe EATING EVERYONE! This episode is one of the great missed opportunities and deserves a do-over.

Series Mythology

-Actor/Puppeteer Jason Hoply was the man behind (or inside) the blob, and will return again as the Toxic Creep for season three's "A Shocker on Shock Street", and as assorted horrors in the two-parter "On Day at Horrorland".

EP.43:
"Night of the Living Dummy 3 Pt.1"
Airdate: July 20, 1997
Written by: Neal Shusterman
Directed by: Timothy Bond
Based on the Goosebumps book: Night of the Living Dummy 3 (#40)

Guest Cast

Erica Fairfield	Blair Slater
Hayden Christensen	Martin Doyle

Favorite Line:
"And they thought I was afraid of *you*?"
-Zane

Synopsis
Scaredy-cat Zane comes to visit his cousins Trina and Daniel, and they instantly start to torment him with their dad's ventriloquist doll collection, but maybe it's the new dummy, Slappy, that's behind it all.

Review
Slappy returns… but not really. The big twist of the episode is that the story will not follow the formula of "Night of the Living Dummy 2", where the main character is being framed by Slappy, but will subvert our expectations by revealing that wimpy Zane is actually a sociopath, and has been framing his cousins all along, trying to get them in trouble. This is a great twist, and adds so much to the material, but when you really think about it this is the Slappy show, and Slappy does nothing in this episode but kick Zane in the shin.

Siblings Trina and Daniel love to play pranks on poor Zane, so Zane concocts a devious, almost diabolical plan to prank himself and get his jerk cousins in trouble. It's absolutely brilliant, but it shifts the spotlight from Slappy when you realize he wasn't responsible for all the goings-on in this first half. I'm glad this is a two-parter, because if not then good ol' Slaps would have been shortchanged.

Rewatching this episode takes the teeth out of all the events because we know Slappy is not our agent of chaos. The cast is really good however, especially young Darth Vader Hayden Christensen (Zane), his cousins Erica Fairfield (Trina) and Blair Slater (Daniel). I also must give a shout out to the parents, who actually try to mediate the drama and step in to help and ease the household strife, which is rare in the world of *Goosebumps*, because most of the parents just don't seem to care. In any case, we are only halfway through this story; the real fun begins in the next episode when Slappy reclaims the throne as the lead. While I enjoyed the twist, the shift would have worked better as a feature, but as a stand-alone show it is disappointing to have Slappy take a back seat in his own story.

<u>Series Mythology</u>

-Director Timothy Bond ends his six-episode run behind the camera on the *Goosebumps* series with this two-parter.

-Actor Blair Slater (Daniel) will return to the series in season three's "The Barking Ghost".

EP. 44:
"Night of the Living Dummy 3 Pt.2"

Airdate: July 20, 1997
Written by: Neal Shusterman
Directed by: Timothy Bond
Based on the Goosebumps book: Night of the Living Dummy 3 (#40)

Guest Cast

Erica Fairfield   Blair Slater
Hayden Christensen   Martin Doyle

Favorite Line:
"Never go against the family!"
-Rocky

Synopsis
Slappy marshals his army of freaky dolls to teach Zane, Trina, and Daniel a lesson in manipulation.

Review

Slappy returns for real this time, breathing life into gangster dummy Rocky for added muscle, and looking to show sociopath Zane what a prankster can really do. Of course, his goal seems to ultimately be to turn the human children into dummies, so I'd say that breaks the prank rules of good sportsmanship, but hey it's *Goosebumps* and you just have to go with it. The point is we get what we were promised, an all-out dummy rampage, and it's a ton of fun.

Slappy thankfully wastes no time revealing himself to the kids, and so begins a night of terror as they try to get rid of Slappy by throwing him down a well. However, they didn't count on Slappy having Rocky the dummy on his side, and he returns to display a new power by turning Zane into a dummy, which raises the stakes beyond just causing damage and getting the kids in trouble with their parents; now their lives are a risk. With Zane out of the picture, it is up to Trina and Daniel to take Slappy down, but just like the first Slappy adaptation, only another dummy can take him out and a last-minute change of heart from Rocky and some lucky lightning strikes saves them from a life of servitude to Slappy.

There are many weird elements to this one, including the fact that Slappy's face is way more intact than the last time we saw it when he was smashed to the pieces. Also, now he's basically the same size as the kids themselves instead of the tiny little ventriloquist dummy. Further, if reading the spell backward didn't work, I understand why Slappy fell, to trick the kids, but why did Rocky fall? Rocky only fell because it was a misdirect to trick the audience, and that isn't cool. Then we have to consider Slappy's green smoke powers. It was assumed that he was possessed, but now it looks like he can transfer parts of the green smoke to other dummies to give them their own life, and then use it turn humans into dummies as well; it seems like this green smoke will do whatever is most convenient to the plot, and that's just lazy. I will say I loved Slappy's explosive finale, and can't wait to see how the heck he'll return in season three's "Bride of the Living Dummy" since the ending reveals that Zane, now human, is a swivel-headed puppet man, and may be Slappy's new vessel.

Season two, the longest season of *Goosebumps* ever, comes to a close with this episode, and they decided to bring back an old favorite. Slappy is certainly given room to breath in this second-half, but because he is pushes aside in the first half, these two portions seem worlds different from each other, instead of organic pieces to the same puzzle. It's fairly satisfying as far as two-parters go, but the shifts in antagonists really separates the halves in a way that doesn't really do the whole of it justice.

Series Mythology

-Actor Annick Obonsawin returns to give life to Slappy as the gal inside the costume, after battling a mummy in season one's "Return of the Mummy".

- Actor Cathal "Cal" J. Dodd steps in to voice Slappy when original voice actor Ron Stefaniuk could not return.

-Actor Jordan Prentice returns to embody Rocky the dummy after embodying Hap the Gnome earlier this season in "Revenge of the Lawn Gnomes".

-Actor Eugene Lipinski returns to the series to voice Rocky, after devouring insects as an alien librarian in season one's "The Girl Who Cried Monster".

SEASON THREE*
Original airdate:
September 6, 1997 – May 16, 1998

*Season Three was retitled *Ultimate Goosebumps* and the opening sequence was changed dramatically, featuring footage from season three and a snappier rendition of the theme song.

EP.45:

"Shocker on Shock Street"

<u>Airdate</u>: September 6, 1997

<u>Written by</u>: Dan Angel & Billy Brown

<u>Directed by</u>: Randy Bradshaw

<u>Based on the Goosebumps book</u>: A Shocker on Shock Street (#35)

Guest Cast

Brooke Nevin	Ben Cook
Eric Peterson	Karen Nickerson

Favorite Line:

"If you get into trouble, use these laser guns."

-Mr. Wright

Synopsis

Brooke, and her pal Marty, visits the movie studio where her dad works, and are invited to be the first riders on the horror studio's tour, but when the ride goes off the rails the real horror begins.

Review

    This episode was a blast and a really fun way to open up season three and celebrate the history of the show so far at the same time. If you've ever wondered what it would be like to go behind the scenes on a *Goosebumps* episode, then buckle up into our tramcar, and join me on Shock Street, because that's what this episode feels like.

    Brooke's dad is the makeup FX genius behind the great horror movie classics from Shocker studios. She brings her pal Marty by one day to show him around, and they end up becoming guinea pigs for a dark ride themed around the Shocker studios monsters. The ride looks like a carnival cheapie with a budget, but when it breaks down, they have no other option than to climb out of the tram and look for an exit. Of course, this proves harder than it sounds, because the animatronic monsters have seemingly come to life.

Now Brooke and Marty must battle a toxic creep and a piranha man while searching for way out.

    If this wasn't based on a book, I would assume the writers ran out of ideas and decided to just use what they had and create something original. This is a real meta episode; for example, the opening scene showcases a couple of familiar faces in the special FX room including a few of the Haunted Masks, the snake person mask from "The Girl Who Cried Monster", the Mummy from both mummy episodes, the alien reptiles from "Calling All Creeps", the Piranha Person that would be later used in season four's two-parter, and series finale, "Deep Trouble", and maybe a few more I may have missed. The ride even warns Brooke and Marty in the following way: "Riders beware, you're in for a scare".

    We must discuss the twist, which reveals that Brooke and Marty are robots, created by Mr. Wright, like the rest of the monsters on the tour. It's not too far out of a stretch to buy this ending, and it works in the context of the story while explaining why Brooke's "dad" was acting so weird in the beginning. There are a few logic problems with this like: why would Mr. Wright give them laser guns to defend themselves, and why did he try to scare them in the beginning if they were robots that worked for him, and scaring them wouldn't accomplish anything? Maybe he was just testing the software? The ending here is different from the book because the robot kids get their revenge on their puppet master creator, and who knows who's going to handle the FX when he's gone. All in all, this is a fast-paced and very fun episode that kicks off our new season on the right foot!

Series Mythology

    -Actor Ben Cook ends his run on the series here after appearing in season one's "Piano Lessons Can Be Murder" and season two's "Welcome to Dead House".

    -Actor/Special FX Artist and the voice of Slappy, Ron Stefaniuk, appears here as the dreaded Piranha Person. He will return to voice Slappy, for his final appearance in the series, later this season in "Bride of the Living Dummy".

-Actor Jason Hopley returns after puppeteering the blob monster in last season's "The Blob that Ate Everyone" to don the Toxic Creep costume and attack Marty. We will see him later this season as "assorted horrors" (according to IMDB.com) in "One Day at Horrorland", another theme park set horror tale.

EP.46:
"My Best Friend Is Invisible"
Airdate: September 8, 1997
Written by: Scott Peters
Directed by: William Fruet
Based on the Goosebumps book: My Best Friend Is Invisible (#57)

Guest Cast
Jon Davey	Dalene Irvine
Darcy Weir	Ted Simonett

Favorite Line:
"A human?"
-Sam

Synopsis
After breaking into a haunted house, Sam has the ghost follow him home and try to befriend him, but this ghostly new friendship may be more of a nightmare for both of them than anything else.

Review
There's no way to sugarcoat this, so I'm just going to be honest. This was the lamest episode yet in the entire *Goosebumps* series. A while back I tried to give an analogy that explained how the *Goosebumps* twist worked to usually undermine the genuine plot in favor of shocks for shock's sake. I asked you to remember the film *The Sixth Sense* and the big reveal at the end that Bruce Willis was a ghost the whole time; then I wanted you to imagine how you would feel if in the last minute they revealed the whole movie took place on a different planet just because. It would ruin it, right? This is exactly what happens here.

Sam and his pal Roxanne break into a haunted house and the ghost that resides there decides to follow Sam home and become his pal. At this point we assume the ghost, known as Brent, is technically invisible, but is really a ghost so not technically an invisible kid. I started wondering why the heck it would be titled the way it was, until the friendship breaks down and thanks to Sam's parents we realize that Brent is in fact invisible, and not a ghost. Ok, fine, good twist. But here is the kicker that makes the whole thing ridiculous: Sam and his parents are hair-faced aliens that eat humans, and Brent is the last human on the planet, who had been somehow turned invisible to hide from the dangerous invading aliens. Say what? That's completely ludicrous, because it is just too much and swamps any believability in the story we are asked to swallow. Even my ten-year-old daughter turned to me with a look of confusion on her face and asked me "What the heck? Why would they do that?"

Those are exactly my sentiments as well. At no time were Sam and Brent "best friends", or friends at all really, and if Brent knew Sam was an alien that would eat him if discovered then why the heck would he want to make friends with Sam? Also if everyone was a hair-faced aliens, why did they have human faces, and why did they feel they needed to wear them around on a day to day basis if there are no humans around to trick. The answer is that this whole episode was constructed to trick the audience, and as we have demonstrated in the past, it never works and it impacts the narrative negatively. I actually loved this episode's pace and tone up until the last two minutes when it basically flash-flooded itself into the toilet with its super goofball ending. This episode should stay invisible.

<u>Series Mythology</u>

-Actor K. Trevor Wilson returns to the series in another unnamed role after appearing in season two's "Haunted Mask 2".

-In one scene, Sam is watching footage from season two's "Scarecrow Walks at Midnight" on the TV.

-Hedge House is a repurposed set that was last seen in "Vampire Breath", "Don't Wake Mummy", and the staircase was also used in "Welcome to Dead House" and "How to Kill a Monster".

EP.47:
"The House of No Return"
Airdate: September 13, 1997
Written by: Dan Angel & Billy Brown
Directed by: William Fruet
Based on the Goosebumps book: "The House of No Return" (*Tales to Give You Goosebumps*)

Guest Cast

Jeff Davis	Robin Weekes
Lauren Annis	Matt Redman

Favorite Line:
"I'm a chicken, La-di-da!"
-Nathan

Synopsis

A trio of bullies calling themselves Danger Incorporated tries to initiate the new kid in town by locking him up in the local haunted house, but when he doesn't exit they go in to see what happened to him and end up falling prey to the horrors they subjected him too.

Review

I'm shocked. I'm stunned. I'm utterly flabbergasted. We finally get a fairly straightforward episode with no major swerves that change the genre or the narrative whatsoever. Here we are given a very simple premise, but it's satisfying because everything makes sense and feels genuine, instead of forced to trick the audience. I thought for sure our hero Chris would turn out to be a ghost or some such nonsense, but everyone is who they say they are from the beginning, and frankly that's so refreshing.

Chris has moved into town and is looking for new friends. He meets up with the trio known as Danger Incorporated, and they want to initiate him by locking him up in a dilapidated house that is supposedly haunted by a couple that died tragically years and years ago. Chris refuses, so they essentially kidnap him and lock him in against his will, and everything that was told to us so far actually comes true: the house is haunted by a ghostly couple and they come for Chris. I was sure the couple would turn out to be magicians or something, playing a prank on the kids, and then at the very end it would be revealed that they were really werewolves or robots, but no, that didn't happen. Once Chris's time is up and he doesn't exit, the trio enters to find him and fall prey to the ghosts. It turns out that Chris made a deal with them: if they let him go, they can have three kids instead of one, and the ghosts took him up on it. The episode ends immediately after that, and I wish we had gotten maybe a shot of Chris looking smug that he just set up the trio, but we never see him again, so there is a chance that Chris was killed and the ghosts are lying, but we shall never know.

It's not perfect, it's not exactly scary, and the haunted house sequence is super cheesy, to the point of spoof almost, but I was just so surprised that we got an honest, plain-Jane story that I ended up really enjoying this episode. The young cast is really good, especially Dylan Provencher as Chris; his easy-going, stoic nature really makes Chris an interesting character to watch. His honesty is in keeping with the storytelling here and I'm just fine with that.

<u>Series Mythology</u>

-Actor Robin Weekes (Nathan) returns to the series after appearing in season two's "Be Careful What You Wish for".

-Actor Dylan Provencher (Chris) returns to the series after battling mud monsters in season two's "You Can't Scare Me".

-The Cuckoo bird from season one's "Cuckoo Clock of Doom" makes a cameo appearance in the haunted house.

EP.48:
"Don't Go to Sleep"
Airdate: September 20, 1997
Written by:
Directed by: John Bell
Based on the Goosebumps book: Don't Go to Sleep! (#54)

Guest Cast

Tyler Kate	Kyle Weston
Amanda Zamprogna	Kathleen Laskey

Favorite Line:
"Reality, who needs it. I hate reality."
-Matt

Synopsis
Matt doesn't want to face reality. In fact, he thinks he can live without it, but reality sees his disdain as a challenge and plans to teach him a lesson.

Review
This episode is one long nightmare, and that isn't a good thing. The concept that you can make reality angry enough to subject you to infinite torture is interesting, but the way it's handled here is just goofy and lazy, and too off the wall to make any kind of emotional impact.

Matt Amsterdam doesn't like the way things are going in life, and picks reality as his nemesis, but the real enemy is his mother's rules, and nothing else. However, reality, in the form of the reality police, single out Matt and toss him from reality to reality just to mess with him and show him who's boss. What follows is random scene after random scene, filled with dream logic and nonsensical moments. I'm not a big fan of "it was all a dream" stories, and this is basically all there is to this story, beyond the fact that reality is really petty and can't forgive a poor kid who didn't know what he was saying when he forsook reality.

Filled with weird music, and arbitrary sequences, this episode feels like it was struggling to come up with material for filler, and I'm surprised that it was actually based on a book instead of one of the short stories, because there is maybe five good minutes here, before it becomes too David Lynchian for its own good. Again, I stress the concept is very interesting, but the execution feels shoddy and instantly uninteresting, because we know it isn't real and Matt isn't really in danger. Sure, the ending is tragic in a sense, with Matt now stuck in a reality loop that is out of his control, but the problem is I didn't really care what happened to him either way. Also, and it's a nitpick, but this story had nothing to do with sleep, or avoiding it.

<u>Series Mythology</u>

-Actor Don Cherry (Coach) is actually a well-known professional hockey player, NHL coach, hockey commentator and sports writer.

-The reality rap and the wedding pop song are certainly new touches to the series, but since no one is credited, we have no one to blame, I mean thank, for them.

EP.49:
"Click"

<u>Airdate</u>: September 27, 1997
<u>Written by</u>: Scott Peters
<u>Directed by</u>: John Bell
<u>Based on the Goosebumps book</u>: "Click" (Tales to Give You Goosebumps)

Guest Cast

Dan Warry-Smith	Trevor Ralph
Tabitha Lupien	Gary Pearson

Favorite Line:
"Studying is… a thing of the past."
-Seth

Synopsis
A powerful remote control changes the life of couch potato Seth for the worse.

Review

Now it's time to review Adam Sandler's film *Click*. In this sci-fi, family comedy Sandler plays Michael Newman, a workaholic architect who is somehow married to Kate Beckinsale. Ok, ok, I'm kidding, we aren't talking about that forgotten Sandler comedy, but the nearly identical (seriously, R.L. Stine should sue) *Goosebumps* episode of the same name.

Seth, a couch potato if there ever was on, gets a brand new device that gives a whole new meaning to universal remote, because not only can he control every electronic device he aims it at, but he can control reality itself. This includes pausing his annoying sister, and lowering the volume of the next-door neighbor's loud lawnmower among other things. It doesn't take long for this power to corrupt Seth, and he unwittingly breaks the warranty on the magic remote and ends up damning himself to a black void for the rest of his life. Not even the voice of reason that belonged to his best pal could have saved him, because he was seduced by the power of ultimate control, and that alone in the hands of someone who considers themselves weak is a very dangerous and unwieldy weapon.

This is a pretty fun episode, with real stakes, and believable character development. I bought Seth's change from chubby nobody to near-omnipotent guy who thinks he isn't a wimp anymore. I loved the western bit toward the end, where he twirls the remote like a six-shooter and the music gets all Morricone, it was a nice touch. The episode mostly deals with the fallout from the use of the remote, and if Seth hadn't have had his pal Kevin there, this would have been a very dark episode. As it is, Seth is still banished from existence for his crimes against reality, and funny enough it looks like he is sent to the black void that we visited in "Don't Go to Sleep" last episode! The moral of the story is that nothing is easy, and great power needs great restraint. This is, incidentally, better than that Sandler movie.

<u>Series Mythology</u>

-Director John Bell ends his seven-episode run on the *Goosebumps* series, which started all the way back in season one with "Cuckoo Clock of Doom", with this episode.

-Actor Dan Warry-Smith (Seth) returns to the series after dealing with a super villain in season two's "Attack of the Mutant".

-Actor Tabitha Lupien (Jamie) returns to the series after dealing with bad magic in season two's "Bad Hare Day".

-Actor Matthew Lemche (Richard) returns to the series after getting creepy in season two's "Calling All Creeps".

-The game show that Seth was trying to watch wasn't created for the series, but is an actual game show known as YTV'S Uh Oh! Game Show.

EP.50:
"An Old Story"

Airdate: October 4, 1997
Written by: Charles Lazer
Directed by: Randy Bradshaw
Based on the Goosebumps book: "An Old Story" (<u>Still More Tales to Give You Goosebumps</u>)

Guest Cast

Kyle Downes	Jordan Allison
Patricia Gage	Kay Tremblay

Favorite Line:
"Don't fight it, Tom. You know you love prunes."
-Aunt Dahlia

Synopsis

Tom and Jon's aunt comes to babysit them while their parents are away and whips up some prune magic to turn these back-talking whippersnappers into a pair of grumpy old men.

Review

This has got to be the most frightening and unsettling episode in the entire series, and not because it has scary monsters or ghosts, but because of the incredibly creepy context of the material. I mean, it's enough to make your skin crawl!

Tom and Jon's parents go on vacation and leave them with their Aunt Dahlia, who seems nice, but is obviously up to no good what with her hammy acting and her obsession with prunes. It seems she's a witch and has decided to hex the boys into aging rapidly, so they awaken as 80-year-old prunes themselves. Why would she do this? Well, she has a few old lady pals that are single and looking to get hitched, so she plans to sell her recently aged nephews to these women. Again, I ask, why would she, a blood relative, destroy the lives of her nephews, shorten their life span, and force them to marry two random old ladies? It is a horrifying thought because not only is it forced upon them, but also these are little boys wanted by older women. Sure, they look old, but everyone knows they're kids, and that unlocks a whole other kettle of icky creepiness that I won't delve into.

This episode is remarkably effective, even if it is incredibly messed up and distasteful, and didn't really belong as a part of a kid's program. The concept, as hideous as it is, is really good actually, and we don't necessarily need to know how the prune magic works, because the writing gives us just enough reality to allow us to swallow the bizarre goings-on. The pacing and direction are great, and Kyle Downes (Tom) and Jordan Allison (Jon) are solid leads that do some great "old man" acting and really sell the makeup; although I think Jon looked the most convincing. This is highly disturbing stuff, but it also makes for good genre fair. Good ideas are often hard to pass up, even if they may offend. I'm surprised this episode made it past the studio suits who would have no doubt found the sleazy undercurrent less than appealing. Watching it with a young audience might bring up some uncomfortable questions, so be prepared to answer some of those for the more impressionable among us, but it is hands down one of truly scary episodes of *Goosebumps*, and ironically it's scary for all the wrong reasons.

<u>Series Mythology</u>

-Actor Julie Holdsworth (Shopper #1) will play a talking severed head in the upcoming two-parter "One Day at Horrorland".

-The video game that Tom and Jon are playing is recycled footage from "Welcome to Camp Nightmare", similar to the video game being played in "Stay Out of the Basement"; both from season one.

EP.51:

"The Barking Ghost"

Airdate: October 11, 1997
Written by: Charles Lazer
Directed by: William Fruet
Based on the Goosebumps book: The Barking Ghost (#32)

Guest Cast

Blair Slater	Peter Costigan
Jennifer Martini	Rena Pauley

Favorite Line:
"Watch out for Lassie."
-Mickey

Synopsis

A mysterious tree unwittingly allows new friends Cooper and Fergie to switch places with two big black dogs who are really inhabited by the spirits of two long-dead pirates who crossed the tree's path ages ago.

Review

Pirate treasure. Body swapping. Ghost dogs. This episode has just about everything, and even despite some thin logic, it's pretty entertaining. Again, a new kid in a new town runs up against the local weirdness, and in this case it involves a centuries old tree, which causes you to change places with anything if you step into the wide opening in its side, and a pair of vicious black dogs, who are actually 17th century pirates. How do I know they're from that specific century? Well, they take great pains to mention it, so the young audience will know the teaser scene is taking place in the past.

It takes a bit to establish the world, the creepy presence of the dogs, and Cooper's fear of said dogs, so the change from kids to dogs, thanks to the tree, happens sixteen minutes into the twenty-two-minute episode, not giving much time for the vice/versa aspect. Cooper and Fergie, now four-legged friends of man, manage to switch back to normal rather quickly and easily. I feel the real meat of the episode happens too late, and the resolution is way too simple, but beyond the pacing, I thought the fantasy aspects worked really well.

The twist at the end with Mickey, Cooper's brother, turning into a chipmunk was a nice, goofy touch, but certainly diffused any tension. Those pirate ghosts went back into the dogs, they didn't disappear, so the threat is still clear and present, even though Cooper and Fergie walk away like it's all going to be ok now. Maybe, it will be, but why would those dogs quit pestering them? Again, my issue here is that the story is over before it begins, wasting too much time on set up, and ultimately this defect lowers its staying power for me. This one is all bark, with a bit of a bite.

Series Mythology

-Writer Charles Lazar departs the series here after writing nine episodes, which started all the way back with "The Girl Who Cried Monster" in season one.

-Actor Blair Slater (Cooper) returns to the series after battling Slappy in season two's "Night of the Living Dummy 3".

-Actor Paul Miller (Mr. Holmes) will return to the series in season four's two-parter "Deep Trouble".

EP.52:
"One Day at Horrorland Pt.1"

Airdate: October 25, 1997
Written by: Dan Angel & Billy Brown
Directed by: William Fruet
Based on the Goosebumps book: One Day at HorrorLand (#16)

Guest Cast

Heather Brown	Michael Caloz
Jonathan Whittaker	Kirsten Bishop

Favorite Line:
"Stay off the guillotine ride. Sharp turns."
-Severed Head Lady

Synopsis

A family on a road trip runs into a mysterious roadside attraction called HorrorLand, a seemingly innocent horror-centric theme park filled with people in monster costumes. The problem is the monsters aren't wearing costumes.

Review

If *National Lampoon's Vacation* were a horror movie, it would come close to what we get with this two-parter. A creepy concept is turned into a goofy, yet entertaining premise revolving around the dangers of theme parks and the win, lose, or draw aspects of game shows.

This time around, and I think it's a first for the series, the parents and the kids share equal screen time, with the parents actually being effective engines when it comes to narrative drive, instead of just hurdles or burdens to their kids' dilemma. After they mind-bogglingly question what a "horror" is, the parents and the kids separate and experience different parts of the park. The parents grab a monster punch, made from the juice of a monster's finger, and the kids take in a few rides, including a dangerous mirror maze and a river ride in a coffin. The mirror maze looked great and certainly must have cost some money, but the rest of the episode was fairly cheap, and I assume it was because they were squirreling away their budget for the second-half of the story, which would need bigger sets. The coffin ride through the wild river just sounds like a bad idea, and I know the book had some other rides in it, but I guess all they could afford was two coffins they could float down the river.

This episode is basically all first-act, which is typical of the two-parters. A lot of time is spent walking around with the family and having them experience the park, but since this is only a prelude to the game show component, all of this seems a bit like filler. I do like that we are predominantly outdoors, which is a nice change of pace, and that the parents are main characters, as well. I don't really understand why the dad let the kids go off on their own in this unknown place, but that's just part of the *Goosebumps* logic, I guess. The costumes are a bit silly (the yellow-eyed one is especially fake), and the whole episode smacks of low budget, but it's a fun set up for what's to come, so let's get to part two!

<u>Series Mythology</u>
-Actor Julie Holdsworth (Severed Head Lady) returns to the series after her brief appearance in this season's "An Old Story".

EP.53:
"One Day at Horrorland Pt.2"
Airdate: November 1, 1997
Written by: Dan Angel & Billy Brown
Directed by: William Fruet
Based on the Goosebumps book: One Day at HorrorLand (#16)

Guest Cast
Heather Brown   Michael Caloz
Jonathan Whittaker   Kirsten Bishop

Favorite Line:
"Darling, we're monsters, but we're not *monsters*!"
-Makeup Artist

Synopsis
The Morris family discovers the hidden game show behind the scenes of HorrorLand, and finds themselves the unwitting contestants who must play for their lives.

Review
If it wasn't for the same cast, this would feel like a very different episode compared to the first half. The lackadaisical, Lynchian weirdness of part one is replaced here with a fast-paced, super-cheesy and energetic storyline that manages to turn the whole thing into a comedy.

It's hard to worry for our family of heroes, because the situation is just so ridiculous that all we can do is sit back and watch, and luckily that's all that's expected of us. It turns out the family has been playing a game show all along while in the park, a kind of *Candid Camera* type show, and are scheduled next to appear on another game show called Raw Deal, where they may win a fancy new SUV, and so they decide to stay in this monster infested world because humans are greedy. Needless to say, things don't go as planned and they must escape. With the help of another monster, they manage to make it back to their cars and drive away, only to discover that the game show host is driving their car and is about to fly them of a cliff. Suddenly, the carpet is yanked yet again when it is revealed that we've just been watching a TV show on the Monster Channel, and the husband and wife monsters decide to turn off the show because they're "sick of these scary human shows"; they would rather sit around and eat roaches. Touché.

This two-parter feels strangely flimsy to me, like it is barely holding together. Maybe it's because the halves don't feel the same tonally, and the feel shifts from horror to screwball comedy. The last second reveal that it's a show on the Monster Channel is actually rather genius, because seen from that aspect, a lot of the cheapness and looseness can be attributed to the type of content that monsters like to watch, so of course I, as a human, wouldn't necessarily agree with every beat of the story. I'm not sure if that's the right interpretation, but I like it and I'm sticking to it.

<u>Series Mythology</u>

-Ripper the werewolf creature is actually our old pal Sabre from season one's "Welcome to Camp Nightmare".

-Actor Neil Crone, who played Blek, and the Host and Makeup-Artist in the second half, will return to the series for another two-parter in season four's "The Ghost Next Door".

-Monster Actors Ron Stefaniuk and Jason Hopley return to the series to play "assorted horrors".

EP.54:
"The Haunted House Game"

<u>Airdate</u>: November 8, 1997
<u>Written by</u>: Scott Peters
<u>Directed by</u>: William Fruet
<u>Based on the Goosebumps book</u>: "The Haunted House Game" (<u>Even More Tales to Give You Goosebumps</u>)

Guest Cast

Benjamin Plener	Laura Vandervoort
Kiel Campbell	Sarah Osman

Favorite Line:

"A compass only tells you which way you're going, not the way out of a stupid mansion of terror."
-Jonathan

Synopsis

Nadine and Jonathan find themselves stuck inside a haunted house board game where winning means freedom, and loosing means death.

Review

Despite this being a knock-off of *Jumanji*, this was a really fun and exciting episode chock full of nutty monsters; like spooky sea captains, creepy old ladies, and laundry ghosts. It's a jam-packed twenty-two minutes of breathless fun, and while it isn't the most highly remembered episode, it is probably the best in the series. The best part however is that there is no wink-wink twist at the end that ruins the foundation of the story, and is a prime example as to why those twists aren't needed if your plot is firing on all cylinders.

The setup is simple: Jonathan and Nadine are lured into an old house to help a crying little girl find her cat, and we as the audience know this kid is involved somehow, but our heroes can be none the wiser that they're in a *Goosebumps* episode. Soon as they enter the house, they discover a haunted house board game, and open it up to check it out, but are instantly sucked in and trapped inside the game as living pieces on a giant board. They are forced to collect items, which become keys, to unlock different sections of the game, and it's all remarkably well thought-out so none of the busy work in the game feels like filler. This is a big deal, because most episodes are nothing but filler, and here we get a fully realized story with well-oiled plot mechanics.

The set for the board game sequences was amazingly detailed, and probably my favorite set from the entire series. The leads Benjamin Plener (Jonathan) and Laura Vandervoort (Nadine) were pretty good, although Plener's "shocked-face" acting was a bit much from time to time. I wasn't a fan of the two other kids, Kiel Campbell (Noah) and Sarah Osman (Annie), who came off a little stiff, but seeing as they are revealed to be the game master ghosts, maybe their acting was affected on purpose. Beyond that small complaint I loved this episode, and it gets my highest recommendation!

<u>Series Mythology</u>

-Actor Benjamin Plener (Jonathan) returns to the series after his visit to camp in season one's two-parter "Welcome to Camp Nightmare".

- Actor Laura Vandervoort (Nadine) will return to the series in season four's series finale two-parter "Deep Trouble".

-Actor Kiel Campbell (Noah) returns to the series after dealing with mud monsters in season two's "You Can't Scare Me"

EP.55:
"Perfect School Pt.1"

Airdate: November 15, 1997
Written by: Scott Peters
Directed by: Ron Oliver
Based on the Goosebumps book: "Perfect School" (<u>Even More Tales to Give You Goosebumps</u>)

Guest Cast

Shawn Roberts	Daniel Lee
J.J. Stocker	David Roemmele

Favorite Line:

"You should be congratulating me on my creativity. Most brothers would have just jumped out of the closet and yelled, 'boo!'"

-Brian

Synopsis

After tormenting his little brother one too many times, Brian is sent off to a special school where his parents hope he'll shape up and return a completely different kid, but what they don't realize is that is exactly what the school is planning to do.

Review

This two-parter reminds me of a mash-up of the films *Stepford Wives* and *Toy Soldiers*. It's a sadly uneven two-parter, but we'll get to that later, because right now I want to talk about the fast-paced first half. We all know school is meant to mold us and help expand our knowledge, but can it change us? Well, at Perfect School change is inevitable, so why demand anything less than perfection?

Brian O'Conner is your basic, jerky big brother, and his parents have had enough. They decide to pack him off to a military-type school called Perfect School, where I assume the selling point was that his behavior would be drastically changed for the better. Brian hates it, of course, figuring that something weird is up with this "perfect" conditioning thing, and he immediately plans to escape. So begins a series of escape attempts that fail for various reasons, until he is caught calling home for a potential parent rescue. The Head Master instructs him that his program will be accelerated that very night. What does that mean? Well, we'll find out all the gory details in the sadly slower-paced second half.

This first half plays like an action movie, with some great suspense and tension. It doesn't feel very *Goosebumps*, because it plays more like a *Die Hard* movie than a horror story, but it's a compelling tale that is well told. Despite the annoyingly obvious strobe-light lightning, there's some really great production value and director Ron Oliver really knows how to sell the space and stage the tension within it. Our story is only half-baked, so onward to part two!

<u>Series Mythology</u>

-The only two-parter in the series based on a short story.

-Actor David Roemmele (Billy) returns to the series here after visiting the woods in season one's two-parter "Welcome to Camp Nightmare".

EP.56:
"Perfect School Pt.2"

Airdate: November 15, 1997
Written by: Scott Peters
Directed by: Ron Oliver
Based on the Goosebumps book: "Perfect School" (<u>Even More Tales to Give You Goosebumps</u>)

Guest Cast

Shawn Roberts	Daniel Lee
J.J. Stocker	Malcolm Stewart

Favorite Line:
"Ever heard the phrase 'go along to get along'?"

-Joe

Synopsis

Brian is punished for trying to escape and discovers the secret behind the Perfect School's "perfecting" technique, which may lead to Brian's complete replacement.

Review

    The energy is drained considerably here from the slicker first half, and even the editing seems to slow down and linger more, as if it were trying to pad out the running time. Gone is the action movie feel of the escape attempts and they're replaced with slow, plodding scenes where Brian is simply searching around for clues.

    Speaking of replacing things, we discover that the way the Perfect School does what it does is that it has a cloning lab underneath it, where it copies a troublemaker student, makes sure their attitude is perfect, and then releases the clone back to the parents, who are none the wiser. This isn't a bad concept, it just gets a bit lazy for my tastes in this second half, and the tension that was set up evaporates. There are a couple of close calls as Brian sneaks around, but how he gets out of them is so preposterous that it ruins any believability in the tale, and yes every piece of genre fiction much have some believability to make it easier for the audience to buy into the tale. What follows is a pretty predictable ending, including the betrayal by someone we thought was a friend, and the twist ending where obviously Brian was going to pretend to be his own clone to get out of that drab institution.

The final moments show us Brian, still secretly a troublemaker tormenting his brother, keeping up the act at home. His family misses the old Brian, but he must keep pretending because his big escape plan now is to breakout the imprisoned regular students back at the school. This is a great cliffhanger that works as a satisfying ending, because from what we have seen Brian will be more than capable of finding a way to get those guys out eventually and expose the Perfect School. As a whole, I really enjoyed "Perfect School", but in its parts, I had major issues with pacing. To often, these two-parters feel worlds different from each other, and that's kind of a big issue. As it stands, this is a pretty solid story, and feels very mature for a *Goosebumps* episode, which demonstrates the show is hitting its stride.

Series Mythology

-Writer Scott Peters closes his six-episode run here with this episode, having joined the writing team with season two's "Scarecrow Walks at Midnight".

EP.57:
"Werewolf Skin Pt.1"

__Airdate:__ November 22, 1997
__Written by:__ Dan Angel & Billy Brown
__Directed by:__ Ron Oliver
__Based on the Goosebumps book:__ Werewolf Skin (#60)

Guest Cast

Keegan Macintosh	Nicky Guadagni
Ron Lea	James Mainprize

Favorite Line:
"Yeah, chicken. Cluck, cluck, cluck."
-Arjun

Synopsis
Alex comes to spend a month with his aunt and uncle in the small country town of Wolf Creek and discovers that the town's name is an indication of its reputation.

Review
    I consider myself a werewolf fiction connoisseur, so anything to do with the moon-dreading beasties is something that I will set my sights on. I've seen some really wonderful lycanthrope tales and I've seen some really crummy Wolfman tales, and sadly this two-parter falls into the later category. A re-writing of werewolf lore takes some guts, but it also has to have some degree of logic as well.

    Alex is a terrible photographer, and he's coming to spend a month with his aunt and uncle in this sleepy little town while his folks vacation in London. His parents are pretty terrible people in their own right because school is still in session, this isn't summer vacation, so not only is he uprooted from his home, but is forced to go to school for a month in this small town; on top of that, they just pack off their twelve-year-old son in a bus and send him off to his aunt and uncle's place and then fly off to London, without a care in the world. What if something happened to him on the bus? What if the bus crashed? Couldn't they drive him over, or something more caring like that? Then to add insult to injury, he gets there at night and his uncle doesn't pick him up until the morning? What is up with this family? I'm already worried for Alex's safety and we haven't even gotten to the werewolves yet!

Anyway, the two-parter is called "Werewolf Skin" because in this iteration of lycanthrope lore the werewolves shed their skin when they change. I think the connection to the reptile kingdom is pretty interesting, but what they do with it is pretty dang silly. Anyway, everyone in town (including his new pal Hannah, and two goofy bully kids) tells Alex there are werewolves, but he doesn't believe them. When we meet Hannah, specifically, she startles him and states "I don't bite", which means she is obviously a werewolf. His aunt and uncle tell him to beware of the next-door neighbors and to stay away from their house, because they're mean or something; so not only does he have a lot to absorb in his first few days there, but his aunt and uncle are most likely werewolves too, because of course they are.

Wandering through the woods he gets chased by something that is never quite revealed, but it is hinted that it is a werewolf. However, this can't be because it's daytime, and we know the moon affects the wolves. The daytime/nighttime situation is pretty flimsy in this first half too; when scenes that are supposed to be taking place at night, are obviously shot during the day. This happens all the time, there's even a term for it, and they correct this between commercial breaks slightly, but the color timing is so jarring, that it just looks shoddy. But I digress, Alex wants proof that werewolves are real, and he gets it when he sees two werewolves climb out of the neighbor's window. He thinks it's the neighbors, who we've actually never met, but because there are two creatures then anyone with a brain would make the connection between them and his aunt and uncle.

The werewolves spot him at the window and attack, nearly bending the reinforced steel bars that are keeping him safe inside his room. This would be a great scare, and works as a great cliffhanger, but then good old logic comes into play and you realize that his window is on the second story, which means the werewolves have to be floating in the air to get at him. They aren't hanging on for dear life; they are flailing at him full-tilt with both hands. This can only mean that we are dealing with flying werewolves. So stick around for part two, because it gets weirder.

<u>Series Mythology</u>

-Maria Vacratsis (Big Edna the bud driver) will return for the series finale in season four's two-parter "Deep Trouble".

-The Chiller Magazine ad for the photo contest features what looks like a production still from season two's "Calling All Creeps." The other mask looks like one from the "The Haunted Mask", but I don't believe it is.

- Actor Keegan MacIntosh (Alex) makes a brief mention of *The X-Files*, and coincidentally enough he appeared in that show four years earlier in the episode titled "Fire".

EP.58:
"Werewolf Skin Pt.2"

<u>Airdate</u>: November 22, 1997
<u>Written by</u>: Dan Angel & Billy Brown
<u>Directed by</u>: Ron Oliver
<u>Based on the Goosebumps book</u>: Werewolf Skin (#60)

Guest Cast

Keegan Macintosh	Nicky Guadagni
Ron Lea	James Mainprize

Favorite Line:

"That's it. No more chocolate bars before bed."

-Alex

Synopsis

Now that Alex knows the werewolves are real, he must figure out who they are in human form, and either free them from the curse or become a late-night snack.

Review

Get ready to stretch your suspension of disbelief, because things are about to get really goofy. Alex knows the creatures are out there and he is determined to photograph them. He stays out the next night, hoping to snap a few pics of them, and all we get are two false alarm dream sequences, which were unnecessary. Walking back home, he discovers his aunt and uncle's jeep torn to shreds like it just returned from *Jurassic Park* and, fearing for their lives, he races back to the house and discovers them missing. Growling noises draw him to the window where he raises his camera to activate what can only be called a Gods-Eye-View-Super-Duper-Zoom-Lens and he zooms into the window of the neighbor's house and finds the werewolves changing (keep in mind that it's like nine in the morning), ripping out of their skins to reveal the human skin underneath, and the human skin belongs to his Uncle Colin and his Aunt Marta, which was no big surprise (also keep in mind that we have seen Alex's camera multiple times, and it is NOT equipped with any kind of zoom, nor can any zoom lens bend space/time as it is demonstrated here for Alex and the audience to get this reveal).

So now that we are all on the same page with young Alex, we assume the werewolf skins melt and flake away like snakeskin, but they do not. Colin and Marta just stow the skins like dirty laundry in the closet of the abandoned house for later use. Alex sneaks in with Hannah to try and free his family from the curse and finds the rumpled, foul smelling skins. So basically, his aunt and uncle are wearing Halloween costumes and pretending to be werewolves? Or are they real werewolves? Oh, they're real all right. But does that mean that they once changed full out into wolves, and then shed the skins, and now they're stuck having to slip into these same old, gooey, smelly wolf skins every night when the moon makes them? Yes. Yes, it does. Pretty silly stuff, if you ask me, and this is silly in a world where werewolves are real!

Anyway, Alex and Hanna plan to bury the skins before the full moon rises, because for some unknown reason Alex thinks this will save them. He turns out to be right, because the skins come to life and he has to beat them back with his shovel until the full moon comes out from behind the clouds and causes the werewolf skins to explode, because of course they do. Remarkably, the curse is lifted and Uncle Colin and Aunt Marta are saved! We do get one last twist when it is revealed through one of his pictures that Hannah was (no big shock) a werewolf all along too!

I hate to say this, because I like the series, but this was just utterly ridiculous nonsense. The concept of a werewolf shedding its skin is fine, but it shouldn't have to slip back into the darn skin like its slipping into a pair of soggy pajamas. That makes no sense, and of course that's keeping in mind that werewolves in general are sensible. Everything from the second-story floating werewolf attack, to the mechanics of the skins, to the conclusion that Alex comes to that somehow burying the skins will save them makes this one the winner of the Head Scratcher Award. Keegan MacIntosh as Alex is quite good, and this episode's writing has a fun sense of humor (watch for the Three Little Pigs pancake syrup), but beyond those two good qualities, this one is so full of bizarre choices and ludicrous plot points that it collapses into pile of goo for me, like used werewolf skins moldering in an abandoned house in the woods.

<u>Series Mythology</u>
-Actor Bucky Hill (Sean) returns to the series for a bigger role, after a brief appearance in season two's "The Haunted Mask 2" as a football player trick or treater.

EP.59:
"Awesome Ants"

Airdate: February 7, 1998
Written by: Neal Shusterman
Directed by: Don McCutcheon
Based on the Goosebumps book: "Awesome Ants" (Still More Tales to Give You Goosebumps)

Guest Cast

Michael Yarmush	Mpho Koaho
Jonathan Welsh	Catherine Disher

Favorite Line:
"Name is Lantz. Trade is ants."
-Mr. Lantz

Synopsis
Ants are nuisances, but if Dave isn't careful with his new super duper ant farm, they may also become our masters.

Review

Here we have another bug-related tale, but this time it delivers both dream logic and 50s sci-fi fun. Dave is looking for a science project for school, and decides to do it on ants after a fateful encounter at a local ice cream shop, which should be condemned. This being *Goosebumps* you know it won't turn out a-ok.

He orders his ants from some mysterious company called Awesome Ants, and what arrives is a giant glass case full of dirt and a small jar of ants. The one rule is to only feed them one special blue pellet a day, but of course Dave and his pal Ben are subject to *Goosebumps* rules, so they decide to feed them leftovers and other random junk. This leads to the inevitable bad end where the teeny-tiny ants become giant, monstrous things like their counterparts from the 50s classic *Them*. Their takeover is quick and easy, and before Dave knows it the world as has been changed for the worse!

And then he awakens! It was all just a dream. Now before you start freaking out that this episode sprang the all-a-dream ending on you, it is quickly revealed that Dave is having the same blue pellets for breakfast. A noise draws him outside and we see giant ants towering over the town, which appears to be enclosed in a massive glass case. Turns out the ants have always been in charge, and his dream was a hopeful what-if, where humans were once the dominant species; this is a pretty neat twist, I have to say. I wish more had been done with the monster ants, which looked fantastic by the way, but Dave's ant-pocalypse scenario is over before it begins really. We do get a bunch of shots of marching ants, but the cg is crummy work that looks like snow effects paints black, and makes the whole thing seem cheaper. Despite that small technical hiccup, I really enjoyed this one. The question remains, is this just a dream, or was it a flashback to how the enslavement of mankind by ants took place? Chew on that, friends.

Series Mythology

-Director Don McCutcheon begins his four-episode run on the series here.

-Actor Michael Yarmuth (Dave) does not return to the series, but he does have a bigger career going forward, having appeared in two episodes of *Are You Afraid of the Dark?* and being the official voice of every kid's favorite aardvark, Arthur.

EP. 60:
"Bride of the Living Dummy"

Airdate: February 14, 1998
Written by: Ron Oliver
Directed by: Randy Bradshaw
Based on the Goosebumps book: Bride of the Living Dummy (*Goosebumps Series 2000 #2*)

Guest Cast

Andreanne Benidir
Wayne Robson

Sophie Bennett
Michael Vollans

Favorite Line:
"I want my bride!"
-Slappy

Synopsis
Slappy's back, somehow, and hoping to revive his stage act again when he falls head over heels in love with someone in his audience.

Review

Last time we saw Slappy he had been struck by lightning, which had exploded him into a billion pieces. When we meet him in this episode, all those billion pieces are back in place and he is intact, so I suppose they aren't even trying to go for continuity like the *Child's Play* series, and that's fine, but it does make us care less for a character that suffers no consequences. Unless there are multiple Slappy dolls? No, that doesn't make much sense either, so instead I won't even try to make sense of it and just accept it as if we are starting with a blank slate.

Slappy is discovered by hobo Jimmy O'James locked in his trunk in a junyard, and when the spell is read, Slappy springs to life. Luckily, no time is wasted and Slappy is on his feet immediately. He commands Jimmy to work for him as his human counterpart and before you know it they are touring theaters, putting on (I assume) successful ventriloquist shows for children.

One day, Jillian and her little sister, Katie, bring her creepy doll Mary Ellen to the show, and it's time to cue the love songs, because Slappy is smitten. He forces Jimmy to mail him to Jillian and Katie's, where he plans to take possession of his bride. We are led to believe that he wants Mary Ellen, but it turns out that Slappy likes them a bit more alive and has his sights set on young Katie. Mary Ellen, a living doll herself, which is a situation never explained, doesn't take kindly to being jilted, and tosses Slappy onto a table saw that carves them both to pieces. Again a fellow doll massacres Slappy. It's over, as far as the girls are concerned, except when their pal exits the bathroom he has Slappy's pop-eyes and has apparently become possessed! This happened to Zane last time, but we never find out what became of that twist, which adds to its cheap-shot-ness. The eternal struggle continues, and Slappy will live to fight another day, but not on this series at least.

This was a leaner, meaner, more stripped-down Slappy story, and I appreciated that no time was wasted. There are a few fun nods here and there, like the phrase "don't worry, by Slappy" written on an elevator wall behind Jillian at one point, and even a reveal of the remains of Slappy's enemies Rocky the dummy and Zane the Dummy from "Night of the Living Dummy 3", which does try to piece together the events of the previous installment, but without any real connective tissue. Slappy is in rare form in his swan song, and is back to his regular height, thank the TV gods. It's easy to see why Slappy became the *Goosebumps* spokesperson, and it's because he has personality and he's fun to watch. We shall never see this redheaded Slappy again, because he gets smaller and darker for his bigger roles in the *Goosebumps* movies, but we'll always have that dirty trunk in the junkyard, won't we?

<u>Series Mythology</u>

-Director Randy Bradshaw ends his seven-episode run on the series here, having joined the series officially with season two's "Scarecrow Walks at Midnight", but having previously held uncredited directing duties for that season's "Attack of the Mutant".

-Actor Andreanne Benidir (Jillian) returns to the series after breaking into a haunted house in season two's "The Headless Ghost".

-Actor Sophie Bennett (Katie) returns to the series after playing an uncredited Medieval Girl in season one's "A Night in Terror Tower".

-Actor/Puppeteer Ron Stefaniuk returns to voice and operate Slappy, having done so previously in Slappy's first appearance in season one's "Night of the Living Dummy 2".

-The movie that the kids are watching is comprised of footage from various episodes in the *Goosebumps* oeuvre including "Scarecrow Walks at Midnight", "The Werewolf of Fever Swamp", and "Welcome to Camp Nightmare"; the later episode holding the title for the most recycled clips.

EP.61:
"Strained Peas"

Airdate: February 21, 1998
Written by: Rick Drew
Directed by: Don McCutcheon
Based on the Goosebumps book: "Strained Peas" (Tales to Give You Goosebumps)

Guest Cast

Tyrone Savage	Janet-Laine Green
Booth Savage	Alicia Panetta

Favorite Line:
"You're history, big brother."
-Grace

Synopsis
Nicholas is discovering that being a big brother is a lot of work, especially when your new baby sister wants you out of the family.

Review

  I grew up without siblings, but having two kids myself I can see what a major headache I dodged by not having to deal with a brother and sister. Sure, there are nice sides to consider in the sibling controversy, but this episode clearly demonstrates the most pressing dilemma: the fear of being pushed out of your family.

  Nicholas' parents come home with his new baby sister, Grace. This is his first time meeting her, because apparently he wasn't allowed to go to the hospital, or maybe his parents keep him at arms length all the time. Anyway, he likes his little sister, but he starts to notice weird things about her, like the fact that she has teeth, and she can run and work the TV, and, oh right, she can talk with the use of some laughably bad CG. She wants to get rid of him and be the only baby, and she just may get her chance because his parents don't believe him. Thanks to a last minute plot save, where it is revealed that Grace isn't really a part of his family, Nicholas is saved from the full wrath of this evil baby, and his real sister finally comes home. The downside is that she also talks and has an attitude, so here we go again.

The horror version of *Baby's Day Out* and *Boss Baby*, plays more like a comedy, than a scary story, but it's at least a very enjoyable story with a really good performance from Tyron Savage as Nicholas, the beleaguered older brother. However, the parents here are written really strangely, and their lackadaisical reaction to the fact that their baby was switched at the hospital is awkwardly inhuman; most parents, myself included, would be freaking out if we heard that news. Also, when Grace's parents are finally revealed, all we see are two extreme monster hands, so how did two creatures give birth to a human baby? Are they able to morph back and forth possibly? This is one of the main mysteries you will never be able to answer. But whatever you do, don't show this episode to older sibling expecting younger siblings; it may mess up their relationship before it begins.

<u>Series Mythology</u>

-Writer Rick Drew bids a fond farewell to the series here after penning ten episodes. He joined the team back in season one with "Night of the Living Dummy 2".

-Actor Tyrone Savage (Nicholas) returns to the series after dealing with a killer sponge in season one's "It Came from Beneath the Sink".

-Actors Booth Savage (Dad) and Janet-Laine Green (Mom) are Tyrone Savage's parents in real life.

-In one scene, Nicholas' pal Sam lifts up a toy block and asks him if he isn't "seeing things", and if you look close you will see a *Goosebumps* "G" on the block facing the camera for another meta wink-wink.

EP. 62:

"Say Cheese and Die… Again"

Airdate: February 28, 1998

Written by: Dan Angel & Billy Brown

Directed by: Ron Oliver

Based on the Goosebumps book: Say Cheese and Die… Again! (#44)

Guest Cast

Patrick Thomas   Louis Del Grande
Jennie Lévesque   Paula Barrett

Favorite Line:
"No! I'm fat!"
-Greg

Synopsis

To prove a teacher wrong and get a better grade on his school report about his experiences with the cursed camera, Greg retrieves it and mayhem ensues.

Review

A smaller scale version of part one, this sequel features an all-new cast, and a sillier storyline that takes the onus off the camera and hooks the narrative thread onto the effects of the camera instead. It's an interesting direction, but files the teeth off of the camera, which seemed to be the center point of the original, as it should be.

Greg is asked by his toupee-wearing teacher Mr. Saur (pronounced sour, instead of dino-SAUR) to write about an experience that changed him and he writes about that crazy time he and his friends found a future-predicting camera that always foretold of horrible happenings. The teacher gives him an F, because it was supposed to be a true story, so to prove it and improve his grade, he returns to the warehouse, which is now an empty lot, and manages to rediscover the camera. Of course, despite his best intentions, pictures are snapped and bad stuff goes down. This time the fallout is contained to Greg and his pal Shari; Greg begins to mysteriously grow fatter and fatter and Shari starts to waste away to nothing to match the fates foretold in their pics. Finding a loophole, they figure if the reverse the images into negative and positive they might be able to defeat the camera's curse, and guess what, they succeed and all is right with the world. The next day he presents the camera to his teacher, who still doesn't believe him, until he snaps a picture of himself and starts to lose his hair. As Mr. Saur goes bald, I realize we were led to believe that he had hair and that the obvious toupee was not obvious, which is what this payoff is all about, and it would have been sweet if I had actually bought the fact that the bald guy wasn't already obviously bald.

I prefer the original to this one, which takes a goofier direction than I would have liked and focuses more on the film than on the camera mechanics itself. Also this time the camera effects are way more supernatural than in the first one, where the camera predicted horrible stuff that could happen in real-life, not outlandish stuff like magically getting fat or skinny overnight. This all seemed like an oversimplification of the idea behind the camera and its curse powers. The dopey fat suit, and the obvious golf balls in actor Patrick Thomas' (Greg) mouth really made it feel like kids on a shoestring budget made all this, and in a sense there is a real charm to that. So in conclusion, while not as interesting or compelling as the first one, this goofier sequel is still a fun watch.

<u>Series Mythology</u>

-Actor Patrick Thomas (Greg) steps in for Ryan Gosling, who played Greg in season one's "Say Cheese and Die". He won't return to the series, but ironically enough will later star in a photo-related episode of *Are You Afraid of the Dark?*

-Actor Paul Brogren goes uncredited, but he returns to the series here after dealing with a crazy camp in season one's "Welcome to Camp Nightmare".

-The names of a few crewmembers from the series make cameos as Mr. Saur's students, indicated by his roll call sheet, and include art director

Ian Brock, assistant director David Forsyth, and producer Lena Cordina among others.

EP.63:
"Chillogy Pt.1: Squeal of Fortune"
Airdate: April 25, 1998
Written by: Dan Angel & Billy Brown
Directed by: William Fruet
Guest Cast

Daniel Kash   Caterina Scorsone
Gil Filar   Maggie Huculak

Favorite Line:
"Pig goes great with lemonade!"
-Mr. Killman

Synopsis

Karlsville is open and looking for new citizens, and unfortunately for Jessica and her friends Matthew and Todd, they've been chosen as new additions.

Review

    I applaud the team behind the series to try something different and strike out on new ground to help the show expand beyond the limits of the books. However, this ambitious trilogy, to borrow a metaphor from the plot of the second chapter, swings and misses, producing three strikes.

    The trilogy revolves around a detailed model of a small town known as Karlsville. Karlsville is ruled over by a guy named Karl, who is... well, actually I have no idea what he is. He could be a genie, a ghost, a demon, an alien, or any other random thing you can think of, and therein lays the problem with this whole trilogy. Our villain goes undefined and while Daniel Kash as Karl is very charismatic and energetic, his unexplained overpoweredness cancels out any kind of tension, because we aren't sure what he is, or where he came from, or what he ultimately wants from everyone, so he becomes an innocuous character, instead of the narrative glue this story needs. Also, when we first meet him he says "Karlsville is open", so does that mean he hasn't been around forever, and this is the first time Karl has managed to start his mayhem? Then there's the model. Where did it come from? Our heroine in part one finds it in her attic, but this isn't a new home, the family appears to have lived there for a while, so no one else saw that thing in the attic before? No one questions how it got there, either? I don't need everything spelled out for me, I like mystery, but when the mysteries start looking like plot holes, then the story is fundamentally flawed.

This first third revolves around the financially-minded Jessica, and how her greed gets the best of her when she is sucked into Karlsville. When a moneymaking opportunity is offered, she shrugs off the fact that she was sucked into a model and is talking to some weird dude that somehow brought her there. He asks her to sell his lemonade, of all things, and with dollar signs in her eyes she agrees. So, to reiterate, the plot of this *Goosebumps* episode, a horror show, is for a girl to sell lemonade at a reasonable price. Yeah, not very scary, is it? Obviously, she overcharges and her greed turns her into a pig creature, because everyone started calling her a greedy little pig. Now, I don't know about you, but "greed" is not a word I would use to describe a pig. Pigs are greedy for food, I guess, but you wouldn't describe it with that word. You'd say she was glutton, because that applies to what pigs are greedy for. Maybe this could have been an eating contest, instead of a lemonade stand, if they wanted to have someone in a pig costume for some unknown reason. So, for me, the whole metaphor of changing into a pig because you're greedy for money makes very little sense. Anyway, she is chased through the town as a pig, and manages to call home from a payphone, and that sends her back to the real world; a human once more. She throws the model away and hopes to put the whole thing out of her memory, but her pals Matthew and Todd find it in the trash and the struggle continues in part two.

Of all the original takes they could have taken, this is probably the weirdest. I would have much more enjoyed a mash up storyline *Avengers*-style, with Slappy and the Haunted Mask teaming up to battle the Blob That Ate Everyone, or something along those lines. That would have been more fun and satisfying. The series *Are You Afraid of the Dark?* pulled off a brilliant trilogy that not only told individual adventures, but a broad story that spoke to the very bones of the series mythology and was anything but goofy and pointless, which sadly is what we have here. But the story is far from over, so stay tuned!

<u>Series Mythology</u>

-The "Chillogy" episodes are the only three completely original *Goosebumps* episodes, written by series scribes Billy Brown and Dan Angel. Season two's "More Monster Blood" was original, but shared certain elements with the "Monster Blood" book series.

-Actor Caterina Scorsone (Jessica) returns to the series after dealing with Slappy in season one's "Night of the Living Dummy 2".

EP.64:
"Chillogy Pt.2: Strike Three... You're Doomed"
Airdate: May 22, 1998
Written by: Dan Angel & Billy Brown
Directed by: William Fruet

Guest Cast

Daniel Kash	Neil Denis
Caterina Scorsone	Melanie Nicholls-King

Favorite Line:
"You're the star. You're the man. You're the franchise, baby!"
-Karl

Synopsis
The Karlsville curse continues as Matthew is sucked into the model to play the weirdest game of baseball in his life against Karl and his minions.

Review
Continuing with the nonsensical threats and unexplained reasoning, this second half is basically more of the same. In fact, you can even call it a remake of the first one because we don't learn anything new, nothing major changes, and we basically get a repeat of part one with a new character.

Matthew sucks at baseball, but Karl will make him a star. The boy brought the model into his room, after finding it in the trash no less, and is sucked in when his baseball falls into the model and he reaches in to grab it. He appears on a baseball diamond with Karl has his coach, and just like Jessica, he doesn't question the situation, or freak out like a human being would, and decides to go along and play the game with multiple versions of Karl and some squirrel monsters in the different player positions. While slightly more nightmarish than part one, this one is still pretty goofy and low-stakes; the stakes are low because we still have zero idea what Karl, who we presume is the villain, wants from Matthew, and what he gains from making him play baseball. We're too busy scratching our heads to worry about Matthew, because even kids need logic. Anyway, he manages to get back, while being chased by a baseball with teeth, when he slides into home plate. He meets up with Jessica, who explains her similar experience, and they decide to destroy the model, but before they can, Matthew's brother Todd is sucked in! There is a brief hint early on to the plot of part three when Todd and his mom discuss his entry into mail-in contests and his hopes of winning one day, and with that, let's see what happens to Todd in the "Chillogy" finale next episode.

The baseball field isn't exactly a frightening location, but I suppose anything can be made scary, if given enough context. Here we are given nothing to work with, as if the whole thing is predicated on dream logic, and that is not a strong foundation to build a trilogy on, much less a single episode. As I stated, this doesn't enhance or expand the storyline, so in essence this could have been a two-parter, skipping this whole episode entirely, and nothing would have been altered.

Series Mythology

-Series editor Robert K. Sprogis cameos here as the umpire. He will leave the series after editing "Chillogy Pt.3", having wracked up 36 episodes in total.

-Blink and you miss it, but Matthew's bookshelf is holding up a whole bunch of Goosebumps books.

EP.65:
"Chillogy Pt.3: Escape from Karlsville"
Airdate: May 9, 1998
Written by: Dan Angel & Billy Brown
Directed by: William Fruet
Based on the Goosebumps book: A Shocker on Shock Street (#35)

Guest Cast

Daniel Kash	Caterina Scorsone
Neil Denis	Melanie Nicholls-King

Favorite Line:
"That's... it?"

-Todd

Synopsis

Todd "wins" a trip to Karlsville, where Karl plans to turn him into one of his plastic citizens, and only his brother Matthew and his friend Jessica can save him.

Review

I feel like even less happens in this one, than the other two. Todd wins a fake contest through the mail, which means that somehow Karl can affect the real world when it comes to the post office, and is sucked into the model to claim his prize. His prize is that Karl is going to turn him into a plasticized citizen. To which Todd responds: "That's... it?" You'll notice this is also my favorite line, because, dear reader, this is exactly what I thought when he revealed the prize to Todd. This whole time he just wanted to add people to his menagerie of characters? Then why would he need to turn Jessica into a pig, or make Matthew play baseball, if it didn't fit into his grand scheme of making more citizens?

My brain is hurting, so I'll just briefly explain the plot here. Todd gets to do the least of the trilogy, because he is given a small parade and then taken to a lab, where he is strapped down and immediately put through the process of being made into a toy or whatever. Meanwhile, Jessica and Matthew realize that Todd has been sucked in, and need to find a way to travel back to Karlsville to save him. Jessica discovers that changing the population counter to add another number opens the doors for her, and soon both friends are back in town. Matthew instantly knows, somehow, that they must follow the trail of confetti on the ground to find him. Right before Todd is put through the so-called Plasto Blaster, Jessica and Matthew pull out some wires and break the machine. They rescue Todd, no muss, no fuss, and escape by being sucked up through a vacuum that returns them to the real world. This absolutely ridiculous ending is in keeping with the nonsense provided so far. The kids then proceed to burn the model and Karlsville is now officially closed, but Karl has survived as a teeny-tiny dude, and the trilogy ends with him laughing manically, but wait until the mice get at him.

The whole "Chillogy" business was highly disappointing. I wish I could report different, but I just didn't buy anything, because I wasn't offered anything to buy. Throwing characters into random situations isn't scary, it's confusing. Whenever a game is played, the rules are learned first, and it's the same with a story. We never knew the rules, so the game was meaningless. I was looking forward to a story that needed three parts to be told correctly, and satisfyingly, but what we are given is basically three stand-alone stories with the only connective tissue being Karl and his town. This wasn't some broad, epic tale that needed the time to develop; it was sadly just silly fluff that could have been three separate stories and it wouldn't have made any difference. To me, and to many others, a trilogy means story growth and expansion, not just the same thing three times.

<u>Series Mythology</u>

-One of the stores in Karlsville is called THE CUCKOO CLOCK OF DOOM, named after the Goosebumps book of the same name, but if you look closer it is covered in movie posters, so is it a clock store or a movie theater? Again, more questions!

EP. 66:
"Teacher's Pet"

Airdate: May 16, 1998
Written by: Andrea Raffaghello
Directed by: Stefan Scaini
Based on the Goosebumps book: "Teacher's Pet" (Tales to Give You Goosebumps)

Guest Cast

Michelle Risi	Telmo Miranda
Ashley Taylor	Asia Vieira

Favorite Line:
"You got that wrong!"
-Mr. Blankenship

Synopsis

A camping trip in the woods forces science teacher Mr. Blankenship to reveal his reptilian secret to a pair of nosey students, who look good enough to eat.

Review

    This fairly standard yarn, with no major tone shifts, delivers some fun suspense with a 50s sci-fi twist ending that isn't necessarily a surprise, but feels in keeping with the universe of the story and the elements that have been set up, so it actually feels earned and organic. It's nothing out of this world, or groundbreaking, but it's a well-told tale, and that's the one thing I'm looking for.

    Becca and Benjy are best pals and they're planning to suffer through their school field trip in the woods together, and together they discover a mysterious cabin in those woods. They break in, as per plot contrivance and sheer curiosity, and are attacked by CG bats before discovering that the cabin hides science equipment, and various bottles and beakers of strange liquids that obviously belong to a mad scientist. After being stalked by a strangely intelligent snake, it is revealed that Mr. Blankenship, the science teacher, has been doing experiments with DNA mixing and can turn himself into a snake. Becca defeats it by spraying it with the amino acids of a fly, but all that means is that Mr. Blankenship is just turned into a fly, and he can now pass his reptile virus to others more easily, and proceeds to do so. The fly-head effects are laughably bad, but I think the extremeness was on purpose, at least I hope it was.

While the reveal of the teacher as a snakeman is cool, I can't help but feel that this episode was kind of dry and simplistic. I had guessed that Blankenship was involved, but he was being so obviously weird, that I was sure he would be a red-herring, and when it turned out that he really was involved, it kind of made it a less interesting and uncomplicated story, which, in a way, I appreciate. We were given an explanation and a compelling pair of young characters, and despite the overly straightforward plot, it was a pretty good episode. Season three closes out here, and this episode becomes the last of the one-shot, standalone episodes, because our final season is only two-parters, so "Teacher's Pet" holds the distinction of being the last of the lonely ones.

Series Mythology

-Actor Michelle Risi (Becca) gets the episode dedicated to her, because she passed away on December 4th, 1997 from meningitis, shortly after filming the episode. Farewell, Michelle.

-Director Stefan Scaini helms his first and only episode with the series here.

-Writer Andrea Raffaghello writes her first and only episode for the series here, however she had previously been a first assistant director for 34 episodes in total, including this one, her last work on the series.

-Actor Richard McMillian (Mr. Blankenship) returns to the series after developing a future-telling camera in season one's "Say Cheese and Die". His character in that episode was named Spidey, so it's ironic that he ends up as a fly in this one.

SEASON FOUR
<u>Original airdate:</u>
September 14, 1998 - November 16, 1998

EP.67:
"How I Got My Shrunken Head Pt.1"
Airdate: September 14, 1998
Written by: Ron Oliver
Directed by: Ron Oliver
Based on the Goosebumps book: How I Got My Shrunken Head (#39)

Guest Cast

Daniel Clark	Richard Fitzpatrick
Dixie Seatle	Laura Press

Favorite Line:
"Kalea! Kalea!"
-Mark

Synopsis

Mark adores his Aunt Benna, a jungle exploring scientist, and when she invites him to come visit her on a remote island he jumps at the chance, but when he gets there he discovers peril at every turn.

Review

This was probably one of the best, and most satisfying two-parters in the entire series, because both halves worked together and felt consistent, and this entire first half didn't feel like an extended act one. Mixing a fresh location with a more adventurous suspense tale, our final season kicks off pretty nicely.

Mark receives a floating shrunken head from his Aunt Benna, the closest thing to Indiana Jones in his life, and is then subsequently invited to spend two weeks with her. He flies off to the mysterious island of Baladora, thanks to his mom needing a break from his shenanigans, and arrives at her camp to find that she has gone missing. Mister and Misses Hawlings and their daughter, who had been working with Benna before she disappeared, explain that they are planning a search party soon. Mark is suspicious that something else is going on and while snooping around he hears Mister Hawlings talking to someone who refers to Mark as a hostage, and he starts to wonder if the Hawlings family are up to something. He gets stopped by one of the sunglass-wearing guards, who growls at Mark, revealing eyes that glow white under said glasses. Mark is then immediately snatched by Hawlings, and it looks like his goose is cooked as we fade out to the "to be continued" title.

I'll review this as a whole next episode, so I'll deal with this first episode on its own. I don't understand who imagined that a shrunken head can float (and this isn't the only piece of fiction that gives shrunken heads this trait), but as a first half it is as solid as it gets. It introduces all the players, gives us the rules of the world, and explores the mysteries in a way that gives us a false reading, which will be clarified in the next half, but it's enough to hook us into the material. Daniel Clark as Mark is a really charismatic lead and Ron Oliver does a bang up job as writer/director, making everything flow and the stakes rise higher and higher. It's not without its goofy plot points and effects, but it doesn't deter the story itself, and because we are given enough meat to sink our teeth into, we can allow our brains to relax and buy into this fantastical world where yelling "jungle magic" will actually allow jungle magic to happen. Let's get to part two where things really get interesting!

<u>Series Mythology</u>

-Actor Beki Lantos (Kareen) returns to the series to deal with more foliage after saving her dad from foliage in season one's "Stay Out of the Basement".

-Miskatonic University is mentioned, and while it is not a real institution of higher learning, it is a fake in the stories of H.P. Lovecraft.

EP. 68:
"How I Got My Shrunken Head Pt. 2"

<u>Airdate</u>: September 14, 1998

<u>Written by</u>: Ron Oliver

<u>Directed by</u>: Ron Oliver

<u>Based on the Goosebumps book</u>: <u>How I Got My Shrunken Head</u> (#39)

Guest Cast

Daniel Clark	Richard Fitzpatrick
Dixie Seatle	Laura Press

Favorite Line:
"Oh, that was good. Thanks a lot."

-Mark

Synopsis

Mark finds Aunt Becca and discovers a hidden truth as the Hawlings family closes in for the kill.

Review

This second half seamlessly continues the tale and ramps up the stakes and the magic aspects, as well. Mark is fed a pack of lies in the beginning by Mister Hawlings, and as far as we know he isn't lying, but the discovery of the Hawlings plan becomes organic and earned later. Mark teams up with Kareen, and she reveals the truth about her father, who was the real mad scientist searching for the secrets of jungle magic. The shrunken head flies through the jungle and leads them to Benna, dressed as a native and hiding deep in the woods. Then the third double-cross (or is it the fourth?) comes when Kareen reveals that she was working for her parents the whole time and they have been secretly following them. They threaten to shrink Mark's head to try to persuade her to spill the beans on this Kalea thing. She reminds Mark about something she gave him on his eighth birthday, and he recalls that she imbued him with jungle magic. It wasn't the shrunken head, it was him all along (similar to the ending of "The Blob That Ate Everyone"), so he calls upon this hidden magic power to break free, fly into the air, and break the spell on the locals, who crowd the Hawlings family into the vat of shrunken juice and the good guys wins. The episode ends with Mark having to take care of the shrunken Hawlings family in a terrarium in his closet for the next several years. It's supposed to be a happy ending, but is it? I think everyone loses, except for Benna, because the Hawlings are shrunk, and poor Mark has to feed and care for these annoying little pests for years. What a hassle!

There are a few other weird elements that keep this from being perfect. The flying effects at the end are super lame, for one. Also, the concept of jungle magic seems to be a singular thing, like an amulet or something. Benna says that Mark kept the magic safe for her, but how could she hide it in him? Is the jungle magic only for one person at a time? She says the natives practice it, so what good would it be to "hide it" in Mark, if it is everywhere? I can, however, look past these weird plot elements, because I really enjoyed this two-parter. There is some great direction and staging here from writer/director Ron Oliver, including a flawless flashback-to-present-time transition that was done incredibly well, and I wish more episodes had had this level of subtle artistry. The episode is filled with great set pieces, including the quicksand sequence where Daniel Clark as Mark really shines, selling his fear of drowning with a gallows humor that I can fully appreciate. This reminds me of one of those jungle thrillers from the 30s and 40s where voodoo or whatever played a small role, but it was more about the characters dealing with the unknown dark heart of the jungle. It's an outlier for the series, being very VERY different in terms of tone and scope, and that alone makes it worth a watch, but the fact that it is actually good and highly entertaining really cements this one as slam dunk.

Series Mythology

-Actor Richard Fitzpatrick (Dr. Richard Hawlings) returns to the series after gifting his daughter with Slappy in season one's "Night of the Living Dummy 2".

EP.69:
"The Ghost Next Door Pt.1"
Airdate: September 28, 1998
Written by: Neal Shusterman
Directed by: Don McCutcheon
Based on the Goosebumps book: The Ghost Next Door (#10)

Guest Cast

Nicole Dicker	Cody Jones
Neil Crone	J. Adam Brown

Favorite Line:
"It's you!"
-Danny

Synopsis
Hannah believes the new kid next door is a ghost and sets out to prove it, but discovers a terrible truth in the process that will rock her world.

Review

This two-parter is without a doubt the saddest, and most emotionally satisfying pair of episodes in the entire series. I would go so far as to say that minus one huge, sore element, this two-parter is the best of the bunch, and possibly the definitive *Goosebumps* episode in general.

Hannah is surprised when she meets Danny, a new boy on her block that has recently moved into the abandoned house across the way. Through a series of events, and some leaps in logic, Hannah begins to suspect that Danny is actually a ghost. She keeps seeing this creepy shadow figure as well, and she connects the stalking shadow with Danny, guessing they are one and the same, until some research into a fire in their neighborhood reveals that poor Hannah is actually the ghost.

Maybe younger kids wouldn't get it, but I think an older audience brought up to understand the *Goosebumps* story formula will guess fairly early on that Hannah is the ghost. The big tipoff is that Danny is the only one she interacts with, and everyone else she tries to talk to either ignores her or a convenient reason is given for why they can't respond. It becomes painfully obvious that she's not among the living the longer the episode goes on, especially with the introduction of this shadow figure that seems to want to get her attention really bad, and the lack of acknowledgment from Danny's friends. Despite the twist being obvious, because of what we've learn from the series, it doesn't detract from the two-parter whatsoever, since she realizes she's a ghost by the end of this first half, so we don't have to keep questioning the intelligence of the characters and can fully embrace the story, which is actually quite tragic.

It isn't perfect, however. Hannah suddenly coming to the conclusion that Danny is a ghost is a huge leap in logic, and she isn't really given enough to believe that to be the case. She does see Danny's front door open and close on its own, but how could that happen? Also, what was that burn mark on the ground when Danny fell? Where did that come from? Were these just there to mislead the audience or does it connect to the shadow figure somehow? Speaking of which, we find out later what the shadow figure wants, so if he assumed that Hannah would get in the way why even make itself known to her? Most of the issues I have with this fairly-solid two-parter revolves around that shadow guy, so let's get into part two to really delve into all that.

<u>Series Mythology</u>

-Actor Cody Jones (Danny) returns here after experiencing Halloween hi-jinks briefly in both "The Haunted Mask" & "The Haunted Mask 2".

-Actor Neil Crone (Mr. Chesney) returns her with his regular, human face after playing a variety of monsters in the season three two-parter "One Day at HorrorLand".

-Actor Dov Tiefenbach (Fred) returns here after being tricked by a magical rabbit in season two's "Bad Hare Day".

-Actor Diego Matamoros (Shadow Figure's Voice) returns her after dealing with time-traveling tourists in season one's two-parter "A Night in Terror Tower".

EP.70:
"The Ghost Next Door Pt.2"
Airdate: September 28, 1998
Written by: Neal Shusterman
Directed by: Don McCutcheon
Based on the Goosebumps book: The Ghost Next Door (#10)

Guest Cast

Nicole Dicker	Cody Jones
Neil Crone	J. Adam Brown

Favorite Line:
"I'll never figure out girls."
-Danny

Synopsis
Now that she knows she's a ghost, Hannah must next uncover why Danny is the only one who can see her, and what the mysterious shadow figure wants from her.

Review

This stunning conclusion is at times a head-scratcher and an emotional gut punch. Logic and the rules of the story's world are futz around with like scrabble tiles and it unfortunately doesn't completely stick the landing, but comes pretty darn close to perfection in my book.

Hannah realizes she's a ghost, and she gets help from an unlikely source: the shadow figure! He says he's there to teach her how to be a ghost. Now, she was able to manipulate physical stuff with no problem in part one (typing on her laptop, grabbing and dialing the phone, opening doors, etc.) but once she knows (and we know) that she's a ghost it becomes tricky for her to grab stuff, and that's just one of the cheesy choices that just doesn't make much sense in this second half. She discovers that the shadow figure knows when Danny is going to die, and that it plans to take his body so it can become a ghost. At this point the whole thing comes to crashing halt for me.

The shadow figure wants to become a ghost? Say what now? It called itself a spirit, so isn't that a ghost? What is it then, a demon? Also, if it can predict that Danny will die that evening, why did it try to drop a 2x4 on Danny's head in Hannah's house? He's going to die eventually, dude, chill out. To add insult to injury, it can somehow fall through holes in the floor like a burglar in a *Home Alone* movie. What silly crap is that?

We must put that all aside, however, because the third act is hanky worthy. Danny's friends convince him to sneak into the neighborhood mailman's house and set off a stink bomb, but he almost gets caught and hides in the closet, where he is accidentally trapped. The match he was using starts a fire in the house, and now his life is in serious danger. Hannah arrives in the nick of time, and not being able to physically pick him up as a ghost, she goes to the piano and uses her previously established musical skill to get the mailman's attention. He rushes back in, finds Danny, and her pal is saved from burning to death like she did. She realizes that's why she came back, and her ghost family returns to bring her back home with them. The episode ends with Danny thanking his friend Hannah quietly, and it sends chills up your spine; not from fear, but from the surprisingly rich and poetic emotions welling up inside.

The shadow figures disappear, because for some reason it missed its deadline, but I don't understand why it can't just wait around and try to kill Danny some other time. The rules behind the shadow figure are never full explained, so his presence in general is goofy and, like I mentioned in the review of the first half, is the one sore spot that keeps this one from being perfect. So let's ignore all that shadow figure stuff and just applaud this episode for being emotionally rich and earning every moment it delivered. The young cast is great, especially Nicole Dicker as Hannah and Cody Jones as Danny, who are the emotional core of the whole thing, and they do a great job of making you care for them, which is exactly how you sell that poetic ending. I was flabbergasted by this episode because I wasn't expecting something so wonderful. It gets my highest recommendation, despite its shadowy flaw. It's absolutely beautiful, plain and simple.

Series Mythology

-Writer Neal Shusterman ends his run on the series here, after writing seven episodes in total, which started with season one's two-parter "The Werewolf of Fever Swamp".

-Director Don McCutcheon leaves the series here as well, having directed four episodes in all, with his first being season three's "Awesome Ants".

-Actor Alex Fallis (Shadow Figure) will return at the end of this season in the two-parter "Deep Trouble".

-Cordina Way, the street where all this takes place, is most likely named after line producer Lena Cordina.

EP.71:

"Cry of the Cat: Part 1"

U.S. Airdate: October 31, 1998

Written by: Ron Oliver

Directed by: Ron Oliver

Based on the Goosebumps book: Cry of the Cat (Goosebumps Series 2000 #1)

Guest Cast

Hamille Rustia	Corey Sevier
Arthur Eng	Padraigin Murphy

Favorite Line:

"Doesn't anybody understand what I'm trying to say with this film? Doesn't anybody appreciate me?"

-Larry

Synopsis

An accidental run-in with a mutant cat will either send Allison to a mental hospital, or the local veterinarian.

Review

    This two-parter is a solid blast, and manages to deliver a storyline that is pretty goofy, but believable enough within the context of the world for us to completely accept it. This ferocious feline fable is full of out-there concepts, but it somehow all works well together like some crazy, delicious stew.

    Taking place on the most stereotypical movie set in history, uppity actress Allison Rogers is in the middle of production on a movie called *Cry of the Cat*. During lunch one day, she is riding her bike, going over her lines, when she takes her attention off the road for a moment and manages to run over a cat. The cat disappears, but she feels bad, so she approaches the closest house and tells a little girl there that she might have hit her cat. She warns Allison that Rip, her cat, isn't like regular cats and that she has to leave immediately. That little girl was right, because a mutant cat starts to stalk poor Allison, jumping out of various places and managing to scratch her arm, leaving green slashes behind. The scratch makes her feel funny and she starts acting like a common housecat, which leads to this first half's conclusion where a shiny object compels her to paw at, causing her to fall from a great height.

 This first half is really, really fun, and while at first I was bothered by Rip's look, when the full story is revealed his look made sense and was no longer an issue. I actually became pretty intrigued with the cat movie they were making, and I actually want to see that one. I know I'll never get to, so luckily the episode is enough to replace the loss. Hamille Rustia as Allison is a really great leading lady, but the standout for me was Arthur Eng as Larry the ego maniac director. As a director myself, I would like to defend my craft and state that not all directors are that ego maniacal, but yes, there are a few like this out there. One element that I found super goofy was that Allison coincidentally had a collection of mouse figurines, which would obviously attract a cat, and it's this kind of on-the-nose characterization that makes things a bit to silly from time to time. This first episode is a perfect first act and first half of a second act. It delivers the goods and is never boring, so what else could you ask for?

<u>Series Mythology</u>

 -Writer/director Ron Oliver will return for an uncredited rewrite on the final two-parter next episode, but his official swan song is with this episode. He leaves the series here having directed sixteen episodes, starting all the way back in season one with the two-parter "Welcome to Camp Nightmare".

 -When Allison's script for the movie falls on the ground we get a clear shot of the cover and it looks like the script for this episode because it reads: **Goosebumps IV** (meaning season 4, I assume) **"Cry of the cat" Part 1**. It's also way smaller than a feature script would be. A musical sting from the theme song accompanies it, so I'm guessing it was all done as a meta in-joke.

-The walls of the studio where the cat movie is being filmed is plastered with *Goosebumps* ephemera, which includes the bus ad from "Attack of the Mutant" and the "One Day in HorrorLand" HorrorLand sign.

<u>EP.72:</u>
"<u>Cry of the Cat: Part 2</u>"
<u>Airdate</u>: October 31, 1998
<u>Written by:</u> Ron Oliver
<u>Directed by:</u> Ron Oliver
<u>Based on the Goosebumps book:</u> <u>Cry of the Cat</u> (Goosebumps Series 2000 #1)

<u>Guest Cast</u>

Hamille Rustia   Corey Sevier
Arthur Eng   Padraigin Murphy

<u>Favorite Line:</u>
"Larry, how am I supposed to act when you want me to walk at the same time?"
-Allison's Stand-in

<u>Synopsis</u>
Allison teams up with her co-star Ryan to find out what Rip is, and discover that the effects of the cat's scratches may lead to more than a fever.

<u>Review</u>
    Allison lands on all fours and this two-parter keeps chugging along with a steady pace toward some really satisfying exposition. Delivering on the promise of a monster mash, we get a full throttle science-gone-wrong tale, with some questionable makeup and some solid performances.
    Allison is sent to a hospital for a checkup, but when the cat follows her there she decides to escape and head back to Crystal's, the girl who warned her about Rip to begin with. She explains what's happened and Crystal states that the cat has lost eight of its nine lives and only has one left, but she can't let him scratch her, because he wants her life force and that's how he'll take it. Allison heads to the pet graveyard, where Rip was originally buried, in the hopes of finding it before it finds her, but when the

actors shooting there accidentally dig up its grave, it somehow unleashes the demon mutant cat yet again. Crystal arrives and leads Allison and Ryan back to her place, where they meet her mother, who has been hideously mutated into a half-woman/half-cat thing thanks to Rip. She explains that she was a scientist who pushed her experiments too far and now she plans to set Rip on the young actors. Thanks to some quick thinking, Allison tricks Rip into swallowing some weird chemicals and it blows the thing to kingdom come. In a cheesy, unexplainable turn of fate, Crystal's mom is instantly cured, too. The mutant cat is dead, the movie gets finished, and all is well in the world with one less cat in it.

At one point, Crystal's terribly disfigured mom says her disfigurement is not so bad and that you get used to it. Not so bad? You get used to it? No way, my friends, it's worse than bad! No one could ever get used to looking like that, much less living like that. But I digress, the point is that the dodgy makeup on the mom is the silliest thing this episode offers, and that's including the mutant cat! That is a compliment, because this is a pretty bizarre tale, but it has just enough of a grounding in reality that it doesn't stretch my suspension of disbelief too far. I love a good old-fashioned monster story, and this was a really fun one. The episode tries to toss in a final twist, which doesn't make much sense, but I feel that was done more as a wink-wink than as a serious portion of the tale... or at least that's what I'd like to believe. Regardless, this feline fear story lands on all its paws for me.

<u>Series Mythology</u>

-Actor Hamille Rustia (Allison) returns to the series after trick or treating in season two's "The Haunted Mask 2", and trying to stop an invasion of reptiles in season two's "Calling All Creeps!"

-Actor Corey Sevier (Ryan) returns to the series after traveling through time in season one's two-parter "A Night in Terror Tower".

-Diana Salvatore (Eve) and Colleen Williams (Nurse Fruett) return to the series after their brief appearances in season two's "Calling All Creeps!"

EP.73:
"Deep Trouble Pt.1"
Airdate: November 16, 1998
Written by: Jessica Scott & Mike Wollaeger
Directed by: William Fruet
Based on the Goosebumps book: Deep Trouble (Goosebumps #19)
Guest Cast

Laura Vandervoort	Tod Fennell
Paul Miller	Mark Ellis

Favorite Line:
"Have a nice life. What's left of it."
-Ritter

Synopsis

While on a boring summer vacation stay with their scientist uncle, Sheena and Billy Deep discover that his experiments may have gotten out of hand, and now their dull summer may become their last.

Review

This finale two-parter for the series is another fish-out-of-water (pun intended) tale, with Billy and Sheena Deep spending an entire summer at their Uncle Harold's, who is some kind of marine biologist. This fishy tale offers us a fresh setting and a plot that continually unfolds in interesting ways, giving us a pretty fun send off.

The kids aren't having a great time at Uncle Harold's, until they discover a giant shark tooth in the sand. They attempt to show it to their uncle, who isn't around, so they decide to monkey around with some of his chemicals and accidentally enlarge a blowfish to fifty times its size, and must dodge its poison quills. This happens fairly early on, and I was frankly taken by surprise. I wasn't expecting such overt monster stuff right at the beginning, but luckily this episode doesn't tease us as much as some other two-parters. They survive the giant blowfish, only to learn that their uncle has developed this compound called D-13 that makes fish larger, in the hopes of curing world hunger. This is amazing stuff, but it hasn't been tested on humans yet, so who knows what would happen if someone ate a fish that was grown by the chemicals. So you know immediately where this tale is going. When a shipwrecked man crawls onto the shore in front of the kids, they bring him to their uncle, and it becomes obvious that D-13 has gotten out and maybe the shark that the giant tooth belonged to is out there causing damage. They all head out to a nearby island, looking for survivors of the shipwreck, only to be stranded by Ritter, Uncle Harold's assistant, who has secretly been experimenting on humans behind his back, and wants to keep the chemical and the research for himself. Finding themselves on the island, they aren't sure what their next move is, but one thing's for sure, they aren't alone.

This first half gives us exactly what we need in terms of set up and development. We don't get to see any fish people until the next one, and then the science gets a little wobbly, but this first section is pretty solid and suspenseful. The young cast is great, but the standout is the sneering maid Janet, played by Maria Vacratsis, who adds some extra menace to the proceedings. This episode plays like a classic 30s and 40s monster movie; a kid-version of *The Island of Dr. Moreau*, and that's just fine by me!

<u>Series Mythology</u>

-Director William Fruet's twenty-seventh and final episode for the series.

-Co-Writer Jessica Scott's first and only episodes for the series, but ironically enough in 2018 she wrote another deep sea horror tale with the film *Deep Blue Sea 2*.

-Co-Writer Mike Wollaeger's first and only episodes for the series, but he did co-write the *X-Files* episode "Schizogeny", with Jessica Scott, previous to this.

EP.74:
"Deep Trouble Pt.2"

<u>Airdate</u>: November 16, 1998
<u>Written by:</u> Jessica Scott & Mike Wollaeger
<u>Directed by:</u> William Fruet
<u>Based on the Goosebumps book</u>: <u>Deep Trouble</u> (Goosebumps #19)

Guest Cast

Laura Vandervoort	Tod Fennell
Paul Miller	Mark Ellis

Favorite Line:

"I couldn't be better. I haven't got a fin or scale on me. But I've kind of lost my taste for seafood, though."

-Luis

Synopsis

Trapped on a remote island, the Deep family finally comes face to face with the slimy, and giant things lurking in wait in the shadows.

Review

This second half goes full whack-a-doodle with giant crabs and fish people up the kazoo. The science also suffers, because it makes the whole thing less believable (as far as *Goosebumps* can be believable), but if you can look past the nonsense, it's strong enough to swim upstream and bring the series to a close with a bang.

Ritter's experiments are looking for revenge and Uncle Harold and his niece and nephew are on the menu. The fishmen are straight out of *Dr. Moreau*, but we then see that D-13 not only turns humans into a fish, and different fish for some reason, but it also makes normal animals gigantic, which was the intended purpose. A drug that can cause different, random things stretches our disbelief, but at this point who cares, because it's a blast. Sure, it can make crabs the size of double-decker buses, and turn a boy into a half-man/ half-octopus, but the point is that D-13 works, so hooray for science. Billy and Sheena team up with Luis, the aforementioned octopus boy, who used to work for Ritter and Uncle Harold, and he takes them to the lair of the fishmen where Harold is about to be sacrificed to science. All Sheena has to do is calmly explain who is responsible, and the problem is quickly solved. They sick the fishmen on Ritter, and he disappears. Harold is able to whip up an antidote and Luis and the others are returned to normal, and presumably the giant animals will shrink back to size once they are treated. We later find out that Uncle Harold lost his maid Janet, because she's become an entrepreneur and opened up a freak show with only one attraction, and that's the fish-faced Ritter, alive and not so well.

The second half goes off the rails, but rights itself well enough with some solid monster makeup and some oldie, but goodie, giant monster rear projection stuff. As far as plotting, it all makes sense and connects and comes to a satisfying conclusion, despite the varied effects of D-13, but then again we don't know enough about the chemical to know any better. We also get season three cameos from a giant ant from "Awesome Ants" and the fishman from "A Shocker on Shock Street". This was a fun episode with a big feel in terms of scope and is certainly broader in terms of scale (pun intended) than most *Goosebumps*, but it's a ton of fun and a wonderful way for the series to sign out. I can't help by think that "The Ghost Next Door" would have been a more fitting, poetic ending, but this one isn't to shabby.

Series Mythology

-Actor Laura Vandervoort (Sheena) returns after playing a deadly board game in season three's "The Haunted House Game".

-Actor Paul Miller (Dr. Harold Deep) returns to the series after dealing with ghostly dogs in season three's "The Barking Ghost".

-Actor Alex Fallis (Fish Face #1) returns with another uncredited, faceless role after playing a shadow in this season's amazing "The Ghost Next Door".

-Actor Maria Vacratsis (Janet) returns to play a maid here after she was most likely fired from being the creepy bus driver who was last seen in season three's "Werewolf Skin".

-This is the final episode of the *Goosebumps* television series.

TALKING 'BUMPS
Interviews with the madmen behind the scenes!

Cathal Dodd

Rick Drew

Brian R.R. Hebb

Steve Levitan

Ron Oliver

Cathal Dodd
Voice Actor, *Slappy in "Night of the Living Dummy 3"*

Jose: Cathal, tell use how you got into voice acting?

Cathal: I am a singer/actor (TV/stage/live bands) and was a very busy jingle singer. One of my jingle clients asked if I would do a v/o which lead to more v/o work. Shortly after starting into voice-overs I got a call from a casting agent who thought that I would do well as the voice of a character, Wolverine, in an animated series she was casting. X-Men the animated series was cast in Toronto and was originally an all-Canadian cast. From there, more calls and lots more animation, which I love! I don't think many people know that the voices of Wolverine and Slappy were created by the same person. That's the awesomeness of voice-acting - you can be whoever you create and not be subject to the physical boundaries of being visible. Bart Simpson was voiced by a very talented woman! How amazing is that???

Jose: How did you end up doing Slappy for "Living Dummy 3"?

Cathal: I had done the theme song for the TV series; ALL the sounds you hear in the theme song, including the dog, are me. I was then asked to audition for the character, Slappy.

Jose: Did you work with Ron Stefaniuk to mimic his previous work on Slappy, or did you try to make it your own? Please explain that process.

Cathal: I had never heard of Ron S. or heard any of his work. There was no voice reference or audio when I auditioned, so I created a voice, for how I thought the character, which was presented on screen, would sound. Once I became Slappy (TV series and film), I was asked to voice other characters - the Lawn Gnomes - Love those guys! Also voiced other one-off characters in the TV series over the years. Prior to voicing Slappy, the Lawn Gnomes and other characters, I was not familiar with Goosebumps, but quickly became a huge fan!

Jose: How do you warm up your voice to get into character?

Cathal: I spend time studying the script and then when I get into the studio, there are visuals. All the characters which I have voiced are my own vocal creations, so they live in my head :).

Jose: What advice do you have for anyone who wants to become a voice actor and follow in your footsteps?

Cathal: Tough these days... the industry is so different from when I started. The advantage is that you now have social media, which can get you 'out there' and be heard quickly, to a potentially huge audience. Downside is that everyone can get 'out there'. I am an ACTRA member and only do contract work. There are loads of people who want to get into the business and are putting themselves out there, for whatever is offered, and off-contract. So... believe in yourself and push your talent beyond the 'comfort' zone'- stretch and explore. Be a good, kind and honest person to those you meet, put some coin away for the dry-spells so that you can survive the droughts and join/support ACTRA/AFTRA if you are serious about this as a career.

Rick Drew
Writer

Jose: Rick, thanks for being a part of this book. Your career started in film with some high-profile, highly-regarded projects. What was it like working on *DAYS OF HEAVEN* and *SUPERMAN*, and could you share your favorite memories from those sets?

Rick: I was just out of high school at the time, still living in Southern Alberta (Canada) where I grew up. It was my good fortune that these films and others were shot in the area. The best part about *Days of Heaven* was getting to become friends with Nestor Almendros, who later won an Oscar for his cinematography for the film. One of my many jobs on the movie was feeding the thousands of grasshoppers we had local farm kids collect for a scene late in the film when a locust invasion strikes the farm in the story. They were used for the close ups, but the massive swarms (in the days before CGI) were achieved by dropping peanut shells from a helicopter and processing the film in reverse.

The fire scene that follows that sequence nearly destroyed the set as well as the cast and crew. The FX guy was not aware how easily wheat burns, so he soaked the fields with diesel fuel. When we tried to burn a small section for the background of a scene, the entire field went up and burned out of control for some time. You can find the scenes on YouTube – we were surrounded by walls of flame that were barely contained. Scary night...

Superman was a lot of fun – we shot all the early Smallville section of the movie, as well as some of the missile convoy stuff and Lois Lane earthquake scenes at the end of the movie. There's a scene where Young Clark Kent kicks a football into orbit. We did that by shooting a wooden football out of an air cannon. For fun I kept that wooden football for 40 years. Just this fall, I sold it at a memorabilia auction in London and got a small fortune for it. We filmed for almost two months but didn't do one scene with Superman (Chris Reeve) in it. Margot Kidder was great fun to work with – a lovely person. Most of the British crew has just finished working on a movie that wasn't out yet. Something called 'The Star Wars'...

The night before we filmed the scene when Ma and Pa Kent find the Super-baby in the field, I was driving all over Calgary to find dry ice for the trench left by the landing of the geode/space ship. When they shot the scene where the super-baby lifts the truck, saving Pa Kent (Glen Ford), the director, Richard Donner, got down on the road with the little boy and convinced him he was REALLY lifting the truck (which was of course being lifted by a cable off-camera). He was wonderful with that little boy.

Not long after that, I moved to Vancouver to pursue my screenwriting career, which I am still doing almost forty years later!

Jose: Absolutely, which led you to getting involved with Goosebumps.

Rick: I got involved with GOOSEBUMPS because I had written family-friendly shows for the Canadian company producing it, so the producer, Steve Levitan, brought me to the attention of Dan Angel and Billy Brown, the series show-runners. I was not familiar with the book series (my wife and I didn't have kids) but I had heard of them. I grew up loving monsters, and even considered becoming a makeup artist at one point, so I was thrilled. I was living in Vancouver (where I still live) but the series shot in Toronto. I didn't even meet Dan and Billy in person until season three. Coincidentally, I got a staff-writing job working for a series shooting in the same studio building, so I was shooting downstairs while they were shooting upstairs – at one point I had episodes of two different series shooting at the same time in the same building.

Jose: Were you able to pick the books you adapted, or were they chosen for you?

Rick: No, it was entirely up to Dan and Billy.

Jose: Did you read the books before adapting, or were you just given a brief synopsis from someone?

Rick: When the series first started, they would send me the books, or I would just pick them up at a local bookstore. But as I continued to adapt stories over the run of the series, I would sometimes get a galley version of a book that had not been published yet. **Jose: You wrote 10 one-off episodes, and series icon Slappy kicked it off with "Living Dummy 2".**

Rick: "Living Dummy 2" was the first of my episodes to air, but the second one I adapted. I was very lucky to be asked to adapt Living Dummy 2 – how cool is it to be the first one to bring Slappy to the screen? I couldn't help but feel some connection when I saw the first *Goosebumps* movie and saw what a big part Slappy had in the story. Of course, the tradition of the scary ventriloquist dummy goes back to *The Twilight Zone* as well as the "Dummy" segment in the classic 1945 British horror anthology film *Dead of Night*. My favorite is still MAGIC, a novel and movie by William Goldman.

Jose: What prompted the decision to start with 2 instead of the first book?

Rick: I don't know why but Dan and Billy felt the second story was a stronger one to start with. The challenge with all the GOOSEBUMPS stories is that some of them don't have a lot of real plot – in the traditional TV sense of storytelling. Some of them needed more fleshing out than others to make an entertaining half-hour of TV. Also, what's scary in a kids book is not necessarily going to be scary for TV, so that's all part of the process.

Jose: "It Came from Beneath the Sink" is a fun, weird one. How difficult was it to figure out how to make the sponge look scary?

Rick: The first book I adapted was "It Came from Beneath the Sink," which I found very challenging – it's one thing to make a sponge scary in a book – but in a TV script it has to work in a different way. I ended up buying a sponge and making a puppet out of it for myself to see if I could visualize ways to make it scary. To my great surprise, when I tell anyone I used to adapt the GOOSEBUMPS books for the TV series, that's one that kids (now adults) say scared them the most! Perhaps because it was a household object they could relate to their real life. Part of Stein's genius.

Jose: "Go Eat Worms" is another gonzo story. What were some of the challenges of figuring this one out for the screen?

Rick: That's another one that was challenging – more for production than for writing. The series didn't always need creative sets or big monsters, but this one called for both. I was thrilled with how it turned out. I was nominated for a Canadian Writer's Guild Award for that episode. The adaptation was later adapted back to a book again with pictures from the episode, so I guess it must have been a popular one.

Jose: "Let's Get Invisible" is a ghost story, and an invisible hi-jinks story; how tricky was it to melt it all down into a one-off that felt cohesive?

Rick: To be honest, it's been MANY years since I wrote these shows – I recall the episodes, but I have more trouble recalling the original story – so I am hesitant to accidentally take any credit for something that was in the book. I think I came up with the secret room – I had a friend growing up who cut a hole in the wall of his bedroom (with permission of course) where we created a "secret room" in and the eve of the house roof/attic behind a blackboard that was hinged to his wall.

Jose: "Monster Blood" is a hoot, and I assume it was fun to write, but "More Monster Blood" is even better, and here you're responsible for breaking the mold and doing something original. Why didn't you use the Stine sequel?

Rick: As I recall, the second book had production elements that would be too big to pull off for the series budget and production capacity (like a giant hamster!). Dan and Billy would have a better comment on the reasoning behind it. I don't know if there was any backlash from the fans of the books. One thing that's fun about GOOSEBUMPS is the books and the series seem to live in individual universes – some of the stories are very different on TV but they're just another kind of fun

Jose: Was there an outcry for the sequel from fans prompting the decision?

Rick: Because the MONSTER BLOOD books were so popular, we decided to try another story – by setting it on a plane, the story was easier to contain and have fun with. I am sure all that goo must have been a true nightmare to deal with.

Jose: "Vampire Breath" is probably my favorite one-off. Any special challenges you faced on this one?

Rick: That was one of my favorites as well – just a good old-fashioned spooky story. The only challenge I recall is knowing how far to go with the Vampire part – how scary to make it. The key (for kids) is to balance the scary stuff with silliness – hence the bunk-coffins at the end and other fun that balanced the danger with lighter moments. I liked the idea of making an allusion to puberty with them getting their fangs.

Jose: "Don't Wake Mummy" is essentially "Vampire Breath" with a mummy, and without the vamp twist. Did you approach it similarly?

Rick: Yes, a lot of similarities –It's even the same house! That said, I thought this one was the scariest one I wrote – I'm still surprised I got away with some of the scary stuff at the end – like the mummy's hand coming off when the mummy grabs the sister! And the mummified heart, which wasn't in the book. My wife and I had recently been to the British Museum in London, so I was familiar with a lot of the mummy-stuff, including mummified cats, which is why I had one show up at the end. I channeled my love of the old Universal Horror classics for this one. I thought it was very well produced and directed.

Jose: "Don't Go to Sleep" is another off-the-wall one. It seems you keep getting the really wacky concepts. Was that fun to tackle, or did you have trouble adapting it?

Rick: As I recall, this was one I had the most trouble with – it's more Sci-Fi than the traditional scary stories. The book had different adventures that the boy shifted into, but we came up with different nightmare scenarios that were more producible. We used the basic premise of him shifting from one crazy nightmare to another and made up our own variations on that theme. We tried to take more of a *Men in Black/Twilight Zone* approach with this one.

Jose: Strained Peas is yet again an episode where your disbelief must be heavily suspended. What were some of the challenges here in terms of making this creepy baby episode work?

Rick: Again, this was a classic, traditional story – fun to adapt. I like that it was grounded with a strong theme and a good story that kids could relate to – adjusting to a new baby in the house. Plus, the classic 'no one believes me' story. Making the baby 'talk' was the real challenge – I was never crazy about how it looked, but it was early days before sophisticated CGI was possible. Again, the scary bits are balanced by silly fun.

Jose: How long did you have to write your scripts usually?

Rick: I would do an outline, followed by a draft and then a second draft of the script. From there it would go to Dan and Billy to make changes for production or whatever was necessary. I would usually have about a week for the outline, and no more than a week or maybe two for the draft; a few days for the second draft. The available time depended on if I was writing before or during production. But any writer for TV will tell you, the faster you get a script in, the better. TV feeds on script pages!

Jose: Can you speak about some of the constraints you had writing for the series in terms of logistics, budget, etc?

Rick: This is more of a production question, but because I have been a writer for so long, I can tackle it in general terms. When you are shooting anything with children, there's a shorter workday because of labor laws of how long kids can work. This becomes even more complicated if you need night shooting outside (which was of course a common need for GOOSEBUMPS). One factor in adapting the books was keeping the locations as simple as possible. Whenever possible, we would keep the stories contained to one or two locations and avoid exteriors whenever possible. Budget was again not my department, as I was just a freelance writer for the show, but my production experience as an assistant director on features, and many years of writing and producing TV would factor into the common sense of what was practical to shoot or not. I would get a lot of guidance from Dan and Billy – they knew what resources they had, and how to balance bigger stories with smaller ones to get the most bang for their bucks.

As you have noticed about a number of my episodes, many of them take place inside a house with very few exteriors. That's a factor of production that makes the stories more production-friendly. It is always easier to shoot in studio conditions where daylight hours, weather and other uncontrollable factors can be eliminated. It made the shows challenging to write at times, but the challenge becomes part of the fun.

Fun fact, when I was working on the Sci-Fi series, PSI FACTOR (the one shooting in the same studio building) I wrote an episode that involved a mutant pig-boy who lived underground. I checked upstairs with Dan Angel to see if they still had the worm tunnels from my GO EAT WORMS episode – they did – so we rented them for my other show.

Jose: That's awesome! Speaking of working in the same building, was there a writing staff in general, or were all the scripts handed out in a freelance manner?

Rick: The scripts were all freelance – which is an opportunity that rarely, if ever, happens anymore. Most series (even anthologies like GOOSEBUMPS) are staff written these days.

Jose: Goosebumps has endured, and a lot has to do with the series you worked on, how does that make you feel?

Rick: I am very proud to have been a part of it, and forever grateful to Dan and Billy for the opportunity. It was a great deal of fun, and always challenging. I think the books and the series are still popular because of RL Stine. Not only is he incredibly imaginative, but he knows how to create strong child characters his readers (and viewers) can relate to. The stories were never heavy on 'moral lessons' but there was always something to be learned with the scares.

Specifically, regarding the series, I think it remains popular because the production struck just the right note of scary, but no TOO scary. Never gory, but just gross enough to appeal to kids. That success belongs to the production team and the directors and actors who worked so hard to bring our scripts to life under often challenging budgetary and production challenges.

As I already mentioned, while the series was in production, a number of our scripts were re-adapted back into books with photos from the episodes. That was the case with a number of my episodes. Strange to see my scripts become new versions of the books they were based on! I think they are still on Amazon, but I doubt if they are in print.

I am still writing as well as teaching screenwriting at the Vancouver Film School. I am always proud to tell my students I used to write GOOSEBUMPS (other than Dan and Billy, I think I wrote more than other writers). Students from all over the world have seen and remember the shows from their childhood. Other than my years writing on staff for *MacGyver*, GOOSEBUMPS is the one thing that still lives on.

Brian R.R. Hebb
Director of Photography/ Director

Jose: How did you get your start in cinematography?
Brian: I started as a photographer on the beach in Blackpool England in the mid 1960s while I took myself to art school and photographic art school. Having been born in Canada I decided to move back and we settled in Toronto. There I studied film-making and cinematography and I eventually applied at the Canadian Broadcasting Corporation for an assistant film cameraman position. After a few years I became a documentary cinematographer, traveling around the globe with a camera on my shoulder, and a director of photography filming movies and series for CBC television. I became a freelance Director of Photography in 1985.

Jose: You had an extensive career before GOOSEBUMPS, most notably working on the RAY BRADBURY THEATRE and ALFRED HITCHCOCK PRESENTS, which were great anthology shows. How did those episodes you worked on prepare you for Goosebumps?
Brian: My career was quite varied and extensive, from the documentaries I filmed around the world to the international television series, movies for television and feature films. I can't really say that one style of genre or production influenced me. They all did. I developed a great love of drama and dramatic photography, so I was ready for anything. This also stemmed from my childhood when my mother (a semi professional actress) took me to her theatre shows.

Jose: So what brought you to the world of GOOSEBUMPS?
Brian: *Goosebumps* came about via a recommendation from a production manager I knew from another series. We had worked on together *My Secret Identity*. He was setting up to film the series *Goosebumps* and he introduced me to the producers.

Jose: You shot 32 episodes, would it be fair to say it's hard to pick a favorite episode?

Brian: Picking a favorite is difficult. They all had their qualities and challenges. Most I remember fondly.

Jose: What was a typical shooting schedule like?

Brian: Usually we shot one half hour episode per week, 5 days. A couple we shot in 4 days. The hour long episodes usually took 10 days.

Jose: How much prep time did you have?

Brian: Not much. Once the series is shooting the director of photography doesn't get prep time. Prep is taken at lunch breaks, evenings and on weekends. You can imagine how tiring that is.

Jose: Did shooting styles vary between the different directors, or was there a formula you mostly stayed with?

Brian: There was never a formula. However, the overall look of the show usually comes from the director of photography and the production designer. Sometimes individual directors have a certain style but most of the *Goosebumps* directors fell into the style we set.

Jose: Was there any episode you shot that you consider the most difficult, and why?

Brian: I always love a challenge so the difficulties were not with the photography. The difficulties usually came from the different personalities. The most difficult episode was the one I directed and photographed. "The Headless Ghost" was like doing mental gymnastics. Unfortunately, I did not get to edit the episode and it is not one of my favorites.

Jose: Why did you only direct "The Headless Ghost"?

Brian: Directing "The Headless Ghost" was toward the end of my time at *Goosebumps*. The timing was right and I was only contracted to direct one episode. By the time I left *Goosebumps* I was really tired after a short sickness. I also needed a rest and more directing of *Goosebumps* shows were not in the cards for me. I moved on to other shows and other assignments.

Jose: Do you have a favorite monster from the series?

Brian: I really enjoyed the episode "The Haunted Mask". It may have been the first one we shot. This is where the girl puts on a mask and can't get it off.

I suffer from claustrophobia so I found this story very disturbing, and more monster like than any other.

Jose: Finally, how does it feel to be a part of such a beloved series?

Brian: I am very honoured to be a part of good entertainment. It is what we all strive for. This is why we work such long hours, in not very good conditions, with very strange people. I am retired now and I look back on such an interesting and exciting life. When I was a kid I wanted to be a clown in a circus. Well, I made it to the circus and I worked with so many clowns. I had a front row seat. It was a great ride. The shooting of *Goosebumps* was a wonderful experience.

Steve Levitan
Producer

Jose: How did you get involved with the television iteration of Goosebumps?
Steve: I had a meeting with Scholastic (the publishers of the books) in NYC in 1994, when the books were still relatively new. At that time Scholastic said they were interested in adapting the books into a TV series. I jumped at the opportunity and made a deal with them to produce it.

Jose: What was the trickiest thing about adapting the books into a strict television format?
Steve: It's an anthology series meaning you can't reuse characters, locations, monsters, casts, etc. (except in rare cases). That means creating a new town, home, creature, and cast of characters each episode. So it's more like making dozens of mini movies than one series.

Jose: How receptive was R.L. Stine toward the adaptations? Did he give any input?
Steve: He reviewed every first draft and was a fantastic support to the project.

Jose: How did you decide what books to adapt?
Steve: We based the choice mainly on which books had the strongest characters and which would be the most practical to adapt into moving pictures.

Jose: How did you decide which books warranted two episodes verses a one and done approach?
Steve: That was primarily based on the complexity of the story, the ambition of the effects/animatronics or animal wrangling and which might have strong enough "hooks" to sustain at longer length or in the home video market as stand alone episodes.

Jose: Was it your decision to make Billy Brown and Dan Angel the story editors?
Steve: We and Scholastic decided together. Bill Seigler, one of the production supervisors, had worked with them before. They were a miraculous choice.

Jose: What was the most difficult element during production?

Steve: Lots of them, working with untrained kid actors, having to create monsters in five days, and avoiding the "cheap tricks" of B Movie horror techniques.

Jose: Was it as difficult finding new cast members for every episode as I imagine it would be?

Steve: Very difficult. Kids sometimes are natural talents – like Ryan Gosling – or sometimes they need to be told to just say the dialogue in their own words. And the directors have to have the skill of working with kids to get the most natural performances.

Jose: Did you ever have any issues with the censors when it came to scary stuff for kids?

Steve: Not with censors per se, but the original "Haunted Mask" one-hour episode had an ending that Fox Kids felt was too scary so we reedited it to make it a bit milder.

Jose: How different was the original ending?

Steve: Same ending, scarier scream.

Jose: Why didn't the series continue past season four?

Steve: Fox Kids decided not to renew. They were going through some internal changes.

Jose: If you could re-do the series today, what, if anything, would you change?

Steve: Not much really. Digital effects and animatronics are so much more advanced today we could do the same things amazingly better.

Jose: Do you have a favorite episode?

Steve: I would have to say "The Girl Who Cried Monster" because it was the very first one we shot, and that was super exciting.

Jose: What do you think about the enduring fandom of the series?

Steve: I love it.

Jose: Do you have advice for anyone who would like to follow in your footsteps and become a producer?

Steve: Work hard, study the industry every day, and meet as many people as possible.

Ron Oliver
Writer/Director

Jose: You directed 16 episode of GB, one less than you directed for AYAOTD. I believe you hold the record as Most Prolific Director of Nightmare Fuel for children. How does that make you feel?

Ron: I love being responsible not only for terrifying several generations of kids, but also for many of them getting into the film and TV business; I've had many crew members come up to me on set over the past five years or so and tell me that they grew up on my work and it inspired them to make movies too! This is really very rewarding, I have to admit.

Jose: I mention AYAOTD because you participated in my book on that series, so how did GB differentiate from that, if at all?

Ron: "DARK" was different from "GOOSEBUMPS" in two important ways; one, the stories on DARK were all original, whereas we used Bob Stine's books as the source material for GOOSEBUMPS. Also, and perhaps related to this, DARK often had twist endings which were not particularly happy endings. And the tone of the show was quite a bit more dangerous I think than the tone of Goosebumps; GB has a lighter tone throughout, whereas DARK went into some pretty "dark" territory.

Jose: You were sometimes working on both series concurrently, was that confusing? And if so, could you share a memory where maybe you got the series mixed up?

Ron: Not only did I work on both at the same time, there were actually a couple of episodes which were very similar in plot; that made things a bit confusing when I had to remember which plot twist was which. But I wrote more of my GOOSEBUMPS eps than I did of DARK, so I tended to be able to tell them apart that way.

Jose: The two-parter "Welcome to Camp Nightmare" was your first for GB, so what was that shoot like?

Ron: What I remember most about CAMP NIGHTMARE was the

sheer delight in having a decent budget (for a two-parter I think we had a million bucks!) and being able to use all of my favorite horror movie tropes to make the show scary - summoning up my memories of FRIDAY THE 13TH in the woods, and at the camp grounds. Cast and crew stayed at a hotel near the campgrounds and we were on location for the duration of the shoot, ten days, so it was like being at summer camp for us too! I remember shooting the baseball scene very quickly - my first AD was worried we wouldn't finish in time that day - but we managed to do something like 60 camera set ups in six hours, all before lunch! That was a crazy rush, but very fun. I think we also had expensive Cohiba cigars to smoke on one of the night shoots out there in the park; our producer had brought them to treat those of us who enjoyed a cigar…that was fun, except I think Kaj took a deep puff of one (he was 17 at the time, so he was allowed to smoke!) and turned green!

Jose: Yeah, you got to work with AYAOTD alumni Kaj-Erik Eriksen on that one, even though you didn't direct his episode on the former.
Ron: Kaj was great; we worked together again a few times after that on "Beggars and Choosers", and a Hallmark Christmas movie called "A Christmas Detour".

Jose: You got to tangle with the series icon Slappy on "Night of the Living Dummy 2"; was that as fun to make as it was to watch?
Ron: One of my favorite horror films of all time is called "DEVIL DOLL", about a creepy ventriloquist's dummy in a night club act; so getting to do my version of it with SLAPPY was great fun.

Jose: Did you ever worry that Slappy would look too goofy?
Ron: Nah, he was creepy from the start. I remember sitting on set alone one afternoon, waiting for everybody to come back from lunch, and Slappy was sitting in a chair near me, just looking at me. Of course he didn't move or anything… or did he? But I moved to another part of the set, because he kinda freaked me out, just sitting there.

Jose: "Say Cheese and Die" finds you reunited with your old pal Ryan Gosling, who you worked with on his first ever project in AYAOTD. Did you get him hired on this?
Ron: Yeah, I brought Ryan onto GOOSEBUMPS; we had been friends

awhile, and he was staying with me at my rented hotel suite in Toronto (he was from Cornwall, Ontario, near Montreal) meeting with agents and doing guest spots on a few Toronto based series; I figured he should come and work on my show too so we could hang out. We've stayed close over the years, and I'm so very proud of what he's accomplished - a wonderful actor, a real movie star, and a fantastic husband to Eva and father to his kids. I also had another pal of mine, Scott Speedman, on that one; same deal, he was in town and hanging out, so I asked him to come do a cameo as a cop. He never did figure out why I made him wear sunglasses at night. Another friend, Christian Tessier, is in that episode - Christian and I did a series called THE TOMORROW PEOPLE in London, England a few years earlier, so it was cool having him there too.

Jose: "Let's Get Invisible" is a wacky one about ghosts and whatnot, was that a difficult one to work on?
Ron: It was fun, but the technical stuff was tricky. It's always a challenge working with wires and green screen to make invisibility work on screen. I do recall Kevin Zegers on that episode; he was a gifted actor and you could already tell he was going to be a star.

Jose: "Vampire Breath" is one of my favorites. Can you talk about how you approached this one, because it felt different, more fun, than some of the others.
Ron: I think at this point on the series, we were all "in the groove" so the creative team was working with all guns firing. I loved the visual style of that episode, sort of Tim Burton-esque; when we designed the "coffin rollercoaster" I wanted it to feel like we were on a real funhouse ride; that was the feeling of the whole episode I hope.

Jose: "How to Kill a Monster" felt very old school creepy and dealt with limited locations. How did you approach this one and what, if any, were some of the challenges?
Ron: The book "How To Kill...." didn't have much in the way of a plot or characters; just an idea really. So I extrapolated that and made it into a creepy dark house mystery. I wanted it to be really scary - two kids stuck at their grandparents' house with something weird going on. And no way out. M.

Night Shyamalan clearly used this set up as his inspiration for "THE VISIT" but his punch line was quite a bit different. I recall the network was worried about this one being TOO scary, so I had to soften some edges of the story here and there. But I loved the grandparents talking about the locked room: "It's an old storage room."

"What's in it?"

"Old stored things."

Jose: You return to two-parters with "The Perfect School", was this a welcomed change from the one-offs for you, or was it a more daunting task?
Ron: THE PERFECT SCHOOL was a perfect experience. It started as a regular 1/2 hr. episode that I wrote and directed with my old friend Shawn Roberts in the lead. But when I went to edit the show, there was so much really cool stuff that it turned out to be a 35-minute episode. So I asked the network if they'd give us two more shooting days and we'd make it into a full one hour/two parter. It saved them money and they said yes! I remember we were so excited when we got the call on set that we were going to expand the episode.

I loved every moment of that show; I think the script was fun - the book had a pretty solid idea and the story beats were good, so translating it to script was pretty easy. And I really wanted to make that show a signature piece; I pulled out all my "director tricks" to make it feel like a big movie instead of just a TV show.

Jose: Do you prefer two-parters or one-offs?
Ron: It's always more fun to have a larger canvas to tell the story - but sometimes a story only needs a 1/2 hr. to tell well. The trick is to know which is which.

Jose: "Werewolf Skin", for me, takes the most when it comes to suspension of disbelief. Sometimes things work in a book, but on TV not so much. I'm curious how you approached this one.
Ron: WEREWOLF SKIN was a troublesome show. To start with, the book didn't really have any plot; just an idea. The script came in from the two writers who were also producers on the series, but it was unshootable; too many locations, too many stunts, and it had a scene of the werewolf ripping the head off a deer. ON A KIDS SHOW??? LOL. The network

got involved, there were all sorts of arguments, and we had a schedule to keep; finally, the writers/producers left the series over that incident and I ended up rewriting the script in a weekend to start shooting a week later.

I like a lot of the stuff in the show, but I understand what you mean about suspension of disbelief; why wouldn't the kid just tell somebody? When I delivered my cut to the network, they made us edit a lot of the creepier, gorier stuff out; the aunt and uncle putting on their skin and so forth was just a bit too much for the network! It's been a long time since I've seen the episode, but I'd be fascinated to see if it holds up. I remember one gag - in the kitchen scene, the aunt is wearing a WOLVERINES sweatshirt. Inside joke.

Jose: "Say Cheese and Die... again" is a sequel, but with an all new cast. What happened with that episode?
Ron: SAY CHEESE AND DIE had been successful ratings wise, so they wanted a sequel, but in this one the kid got fatter and fatter. I don't think we'd get away with that story line now in 2018 - fat shaming isn't something considered appropriate these days! I don't recall much about the episode except that it didn't really work; the "fat" suit and makeup effects weren't terribly successful. I think we cut and recut it a lot, but didn't really end up with anything that satisfied any of us.

Jose: "How I Got My Shrunken Head" was a very welcomed change of pace for the series. Did you enjoy tackling a different, more adventurous type story?
Ron: I LOVED THAT ONE. We filmed for ten days, in a huge park in Toronto; production built me that whole camp, complete with a working shower! I remember reading the book and thinking "I want to make a 1940's style action/supernatural movie" and pitched the idea to the network - they loved it too.

I'm proud of several cool moments in that show - the flashback explanation scene in the medical tent was all done in ONE SHOT, no edits - we had actors running around changing costume behind camera and running back in again to make entrances; so fun to really DIRECT something like that! And the airport scene was a blast; we filmed at a real airport and the Elvis Pilot was a friend of mine who did a great job! I think it's one of the more successful episodes for sure, probably because it feels BIG!

Jose: "Cry of the Cat", your final two episodes, seemed right up your alley. Was it fun to tackle a meta take on the world of GB, and the horror that it can unleash on the world?

Ron: The book is basically a kid version of PET SEMATARY - I didn't think it had a whole episode in it. But since it was the final show of the season - and we figured the final show of the series too - it made sense to deconstruct the series and have fun for the fans... and ourselves too! I put together a story outline for the show and sent it to Bob and Jane Stine - they had script approval - and Bob sent me a note saying "you're either crazy or a genius. But I LOVE this idea!" So we did a behind the scenes movie, which then becomes a real movie. A couple fun things:

-The opening is our tribute not just to RL Stine's walk along the street in the opening credits of the series, but also to THE EXORCIST.

-When we reveal that we're watching a MOVIE, it's all done in another of my favorite ONE SHOT camera moves - from the time the cat claws are revealed as fake to the moment the assistant yells "that's lunch" is all one shot; it was a three-and-a-half-page scene in the script and we set it up and rehearsed it a few times, shot it, and had finished the whole day's work by lunch. I gave the crew the rest of the day off.

-The director of the movie-within-the-movie is dressed identically to how I dress on set (during summer shoots anyway!).

-When we finished shooting that one, we all knew the adventure of the five-year series was over; we had spent so much time together over the years we were like family   -We even took Christmas vacation together one year in Mexico as a team! So much fun with those people.

Jose: Do you have a favorite episode of GB?

Ron: It's probably a tie between THE PERFECT SCHOOL and CRY OF THE CAT.

Jose: According to the official records, there are only 4 season of GB. Did you find it odd that the series didn't continue past season 4, especially with a brand like GB so popular on bookshelves?

Ron: We actually did FIVE SEASONS worth of show, but the double episodes of the fifth season sort of make it feel like 4. And five seasons is all you need to make a syndicated series (at least it was at the time), so that was all the network wanted. But honestly, it also felt like we had done it all by then - all the stories had been told and anything we did beyond CRY OF THE CAT would feel like we were just repeating ourselves; we did it once, we did it (mostly) well, so why not just finish up on a high note?

Jose: You have gone on to adapt other R.L. Stine works, so can you talk about a few of those?

Ron: I wrote something called WHEN GOOD GHOULS GO BAD for FOX, that I was going to direct, but then it ended up going to Australia and they hired a local director there; he did a rewrite of the script. The Writer's Guild of America (my writing union) did an arbitration for credit on the movie and I was told it had been changed substantially enough that I didn't receive a writing credit. This sort of thing happens all the time, so I didn't particularly mind - especially when the Stines saw the movie and told me I needn't bother watching it.

I had a happier time on ONE NIGHT IN DOOM HOUSE: MOSTLY GHOSTLY 3 - it was very much like PERFECT SCHOOL or CRY OF THE CAT in that I wrote the script and directed it using every director trick in the book. Again, the original book didn't have much story, and it was part of a convoluted mythology from two previous movies, neither of which made much sense. I decided to throw out a lot of the older stuff, keep some of the original book idea, and start with an all new story. It was very satisfying indeed, and every day on that film set was a pleasure; great cast (Jamie Kennedy, Danny Trejo, Morgan Fairchild…!) and my regular TV movie crew in Vancouver, as well as a brilliant CGI effects team. I'm really proud of DOOM HOUSE. ESPECIALLY the opening credits sequence - we built that model on the sound stage and used a super-techno crane to get the shot!

Jose: Lastly, would you share some advice for anyone who might want to follow in your footsteps?

Ron: Write. Write some more, Keep writing. And when you're done, write. WE always need material, new stories, new voices. And when you have a script that everybody wants, you're in a great position to move ahead in the film and TV industry. Everybody's path in this business is different; I've had a combination of luck and support from all the right people which has made all the difference. I've always loved cinema; I made movies when I was five years old. There's really nothing else I'd want to do with my life and, touch wood, I'll keep doing it until I drop dead on a film set!

AFTERWORD
Interview with A Super Fan

I got a chance to become good friends with *Goosebumps* megacollector Zechariah after my book on *Are You Afraid of the Dark?* was released. He is a huge fan and collector for that series, and he reached out to share his collection with me, which he displays lovingly on his YouTube channel (http://www.youtube.com/ZakBabyTV). I noticed he was a huge *Goosebumps*, or GB, fan and collector, and I tapped him for info when it came toward research for this book, so it wouldn't be complete without including his thoughts on the series that we both consider a seminal piece of our childhood.

Jose: Ok Zak, so what started your obsession with GB?

Zechariah: I've been into *Goosebumps* since it 1st originated back in 1992, when I was 7 years old collecting the books. As a youth in school before I started even reading them, I would trade books with other kids in class just based off how cool the covers were & eventually started reading the books and having the school merchandise such as binders, pencils, etc. and watching the TV show on Fox Kids on Saturday mornings.

Jose: Let's start with the book series then, since that kicked off your passion for the brand. What are your top five books?

Zechariah: 1. Attack of the Mutant: Always loved comics, superheroes, forts or clubhouses. I always wanted a treehouse as a kid, so this book latched onto me big time.

2. Welcome to Camp Nightmare: I not only love camping, forestry, the outdoors, and campfires etc., but I also used to go to a camp for kids during the summers called Camp Marston in Julian, CA in the mid 90s.

3. The Haunted Mask: I'm a huge Halloween fan. Love trick or treating, dressing up and terrifying the neighborhood.

4. A Shocker on Shock Street: I just loved this story, love theme parks too. This book was just a great story with monsters and robots, period.

5. <u>A Night in Terror Tower</u>: I for one love anything Medieval, Viking, Greece mythology etc. This is just one hell of a story. Also York is a real place in England; saw it on *Vikings* on the History channel.

Jose: <u>Haunted</u> Mask is a favorite of mine, too. So now let's switch gears and discuss the fallout of the books success, which is the series itself. I'm sure it will be hard, what are your top five episodes?

Zechariah: This is a big difference between episodes compared to the books. My top 5 episodes are:

1. "Attack of the Mutant": This is the ultimate book and episode, period. It screams my name in all aspects from a sense of adventure, mystery, thriller, to imagination. Plus, Adam West starred as the Galloping Gazelle in the episode.
2. "The Haunted Mask": This episode is still creepy to this day, the mask looks incredibly real, unlike the remake for the movies. Carly Beth (Kathryn Long) is such a great actress in this episode, I loved the small town suburb feel to the episode. Overall A+.
3. "Welcome to Camp Nightmare": This episode was so amazing, great story, good acting, great scenery. The camp counselor, Larry, was so mean; everyone hates him, which means he was an excellent actor for that role. They went pretty close to the story of the book, too.
4. "The House of No Return": This was such a great episode, with the danger club members, and the new kid in town trying to fit in and having to take the haunted house trial to become part of their club. It was such an amazing episode with a great twist at the end.
5. "The Haunted House Game": This episode is great! They find a board game and they are forced to play and finish or they'll be stuck in the house forever. This was very entertaining.

Jose: I agree on "Attack of the Mutant", it's absolutely wonderful, and full of great characters. Speaking of which, the series thrived on unique creations, so I'm very curious what your top 5 favorite monster in the series were?

Zechariah: 1. The Masked Mutant: He can change his molecules into anything solid and he's extremely strong and smart.

2. The Haunted Mask: So incredibly evil and mysterious. Halloween's worst nightmare.

3. The Werewolf: Fast, strong, evil, pretty much unstoppable, and incredibly scary.

4. Creeps: Lizard-like creatures who want to rule the world. Creeps Rule!

5. Curly: Unfortunately, never got any role in any episodes or in the movies, yet the main face to most of the Goosebumps merchandise.

Jose: Yeah, Curly was given the shaft. That is a bit weird, seeing as he is on almost every item from the series. Which leads me to why you're here. What turned you into a collector?

Zechariah: I used to collect the books as a youth, which turned into a hobby later on to bring back my memories from my childhood, along with *Are You Afraid of the Dark?* from Nickelodeon. I share that with the world on YouTube. Nothing can compare to the 90's kids TV shows.

Jose: How many pieces do you own? A rough estimate is fine.

Zechariah: To be honest, I have no clue. I have shelves and shelves and it keeps growing. If I were to guess, including the books, I probably have over 1000 items and counting.

Jose: That's a hell of a haul! Among those pieces is there one that you might consider your most sentimental item?

Zechariah: My most sentimental item would have to be the 8 x 10 *Goosebumps* MGM Disney photo my cousin and I are in that we had taken during the *Goosebumps* show in Florida in 1997. It was a green screen shot, where I picked the Welcome to Camp Nightmare background. 2nd most sentimental item(s) would be the 2nd series *Goosebumps* collectible figurines which were impossible to find, but I got ahold of the complete set of 6 over time.

Jose: I remember that GB thing at MGM Disney, which is now called Disney's Hollywood Studios. And I imagine those hard to find figurines weren't cheap, but maybe there are other rare items in your collection. What's the most valuable item you have?

Zechariah: It would have to be the 1999 Horrorland Microverse sculpt playset.

Only 2 exist in the world, as it was a prototype that was never put into stores, because they decided not to go forward with the production, and the prototype ended up being used for an 'Ice Age' playset instead.

Jose: Is there a white whale piece of merchandise that you can't find, but you desperately want?

Zechariah: Believe it or not it's the *Goosebumps* beanbag chair. I have been looking for it for years.

Jose: So now that we exist in a post-series world. The GB brand has expanded into feature films. Since you're such a passionate, invested fan, what are your thoughts on the new theatrical films?

Zechariah: To be honest, they're very disappointing. They have made it so family-friendly it now has a Disney comedy feel to it with a twist of some love story. That is not *Goosebumps* at all. It's supposed to be a spooky, dark, yet appropriate, thriller. Biggest concern is the fact that they don't have enough of the book characters in the films. The 1st movie had a ton of the newer series monsters in the far distance. The Haunted Mask I still haven't even seen in the film, but they aren't using the original mask anyways, which is a total bummer. They never added the Masked Mutant, Curly, or Monster Blood. I mean there're some seriously popular characters aside from Slappy they totally ignored. Regarding the 2nd film, there was more Halloween decorations than book characters. Plus, they used the same main monsters from the first film in part 2. I loved the actors more in the 2nd film but again, *Goosebumps* isn't supposed to be a comedy.

Jose: I personally really enjoyed both the first film and the *Haunted Halloween* sequel, and so did my kids. Maybe watching it with my children helped me get over a few of those same gripes I share with you, but overall they delivered for me, and I know it inspired my kids to read more of the books. I do agree that they should have integrated more characters, than just making it the Slappy show. Now, keeping all that in mind, would you watch a reboot series, or do you think we even need one?

Zechariah: Absolutely!!! Since they can't seem to grasp the theatrical movies correctly to have the *Goosebumps* name live up to it's legacy, maybe a TV show reboot would work out better instead.

Jose: All right man, let's wrap this puppy up. As we close this chapter on the series, what do you hope for the future of GB?

Zechariah: I don't see too many books being made, but I can be mistaken. I'd like to see more promotion for the upcoming films. They really failed when it came to marketing their movies, and they need to make more merchandise, too. I'd hope if they make a 3rd movie they place it in Horrorland, and add all the missing book characters into the film that are desired by the fans and that have not been added to the first two films.

Zechariah with a sliver of his collection. Photo Courtesy of ZakBabyTV

SPECIAL THANKS

This was a labor of love and joy for me, and I hope you enjoyed it. Firstly, I would like to thank my friend and publisher Ben Ohmart for understanding the value of childhood nostalgia. I want to also thank my interview subjects who got back to me and provided all of us with some exclusive, exciting insight on the making of the series: my kindest thanks to Cathal Dodd, Rick Drew, Brian R.R. Hebb, Steve Levitan, and my old pal from *Are You Afraid of the Dark?*, Ron Oliver! I also want to thank my new pal, and superfan, Zechariah, and I urge you all to check out his amazing, breathtaking collection on his YouTube channel: (http://www.youtube.com/ZakBabyTV).

One final shout out to Mr. R.L. Stine. Not sure if he'll see this, but thanks for all the nightmares.

www.ingramcontent.com/pod-product-compliance
Lightning Source LLC
Chambersburg PA
CBHW050107170426
43198CB00014B/2493